Enneagram

The Secrets Behind Your Personality Type

(Understanding and Finding Yourself Through Astrology)

Eric Shaffer

Published by Knowledge Icons

Eric Shaffer

Enneagram: The Secrets Behind Your Personality Type
(Understanding and Finding Yourself Through Astrology)

ISBN 978-1-990084-62-1

Legal & Disclaimer

The information contained in this book is not designed to replace or take the place of any form of medicine or professional medical advice. The information in this book has been provided for educational and entertainment purposes only.

The information contained in this book has been compiled from sources deemed reliable, and it is accurate to the best of the Author's knowledge; however, the Author cannot guarantee its accuracy and validity and cannot be held liable for any errors or omissions. Changes are periodically made to this book. You must consult your doctor or get professional medical advice before using any of the

Table of Contents

Introduction

The enneagram is a standout amongst the most intense devices in self revelation and self-improvement. The outcomes from the enneagram is amazingly exact and tells the qualities, shortcomings, center inspirations, states of mind, idiosyncrasies and essentially much about the individual once his actual sort is found.

The primary commencement of the enneagram started with George Ivanovich Gurdjieff – an Armenian spiritualist and otherworldly educator. His work on the enneagram is truly significant due to the way that the enneagram model has been known since antiquated times however it was Gurdjieff research who made the model freely known.

In the most recent decades, there is a significant move in the way the enneagram is contemplated as it increased more noticeable quality in the field of individual formative studies through these two people – Oscar Ichazo and Claudio Naranjo.

Enneagram is synonymous with the number 9 as the enneagram has 9 purposes of references. Each of the focuses in the enneagram speaks to an extraordinary and particular identity sort.

An individual who has the attributes of a sort one (commonly known as the reformer or fussbudget) may contrast significantly from an individual who is a sort 4 (normally known as the craftsman or the maverick). Inside and out investigation of the enneagram uncovers significant self revelation and is truly helpful regarding the matter of taking care of organizations, clash and numerous parts of a relationship.

Chapter 1: A Guide To Spiritual Transformation

The enneagram is a powerful type of gateway towards the understanding of others and self-awareness. It gives a description of different dynamics and structures concerning the major personality types by creating a path to a life which is more integrated and rewarding. It comes from the Greek word 'ennea' which loosely translates to nine, and 'grammos' that entails a written symbol.

So these are nine distinct strategies for relating to the self and others. Each type for the enneagram represents a different thought approach that comes from a different inner motivation and perspective of the world. The enneagram enables a better understanding thus through universal language which transcends nationality, culture, religion and even gender.

Your enneagram core functions as a home base from which one can make sense of integration and individuation. It is crucial to keep in mind that different enneagrams can display similar behavior. The styles are not based solely according to behavior and outward representations can be deceiving.

In order to distinguish between the different enneagrams, one has to access motivation in order to explore the reasons why people may choose to act in a particular manner and why acting in this way is given value by that person.

Determination of an individual's personality type with the use of the enneagram system does not necessarily put one inside a defined box of nine archetypes. It assists people to see the box from where they are able to experience the world. With this in mind, one can step outside their worldview. Ideally speaking, personality is effective in allowing one to express themselves because they are able to categorize and identify who they really are. At the same time there can be issues when people get stuck in automatic habits. In discovering these unconscious patterns, people are able to lead lives which are more fulfilling and enjoy relationships which are overall healthier. Working within the enneagram model allows people to become successful in their relationships at home and within the working environment. Through understanding automatic reactions and blind spots, people can become more flexible with others in their lives and understand what others are feeling and thinking. This making it easier to tolerate other and be more compassionate. It also helps people to not take the negative reactions or their hostility in such a manner that it is personal. Through the identification of how you are emotionally and psychologically defensive, the enneagram allows you to have a chance at profound growth. At another level it also allows you to develop your relationship with yourself and better this, so that you can become more productive towards yourself and anything within your life.

Simply, the enneagram enables and grows one's capacity when it comes to self-observation. It provides vision for how the healthiest manifestation of people's types can look. Using this detail, it sets a path for the manner in getting to a higher level of awareness. Each type within the enneagram has particular behaviors that satisfy its needs and desires. This is the main strategy of the particular type in life. That would be driving much of what the type does. The enneagram is able to help people spot when they are being run by their passions, allowing people to satisfy their needs in a healthier manner.

For example, the passion for type seven happens to be gluttony. This is the traditional meaning for overeating which extends to over consumption. The people with this type look for experiences in trying to find a sense of fulfillment which they fear may remain elusive. In truth, they may feel that nothing they embark on will bring the fulfillment which they look for to bring happiness and contentment.

Chapter 2: The Enneagram Of Personality

It is not my purpose to present a detailed description of all of the personality types in this book. Instead, I want to provide a brief description of each type together with appropriate diagrams that help to explain the relationships between them.

Personality Types

The diagram to the left was adapted from the work of Helen Palmer. It shows the shape of the diagram as well as labeling all of the points with their personality types.

Type 1 is the perfectionist

A person of this type is always looking for perfection in oneself and others. They desire things to be just right, and in insisting upon perfection they make excellent managers and project leaders. When things don't go their way, they tend to react by feeling resentment towards others. Their primary passion is anger, and their chief feature is the continual striving for their idea of how things should be.

Type 2 is the giver

A person of this type is looking for love and approval by helping others with the hidden agenda that they will be recognized for all the good they are doing and responded with the love that they crave. Evolved twos can be genuine care takers without regards to their own needs. They take pride in all that they do for people, which is their primary passion. The chief feature of the two is the desire to win love and approval by making themselves indispensable to others.

Type 3 is the performer

A person of this type is result-oriented and pushes themself to accomplish tasks and reap the benefits of the good life. Threes are good chameleons, which works both ways to cause them to deceive themselves and others. They make good leaders and accomplish a lot for the benefit of their image. Their primary passion is self-deception, and their chief feature is making things happen that make them look good.

Type 4 is the romantic

A person of this type is primarily concerned with the intensity of life, especially in relationships. They consider themselves to be very special and are attracted to the sensual and artistic. They can be very supportive in helping friends through painful situations. The primary passion for a four is an attraction to melancholy and the chief feature of a four is his or her preoccupation with longing for things to be other than they are.

Type 5 is the observer

A person of this type is concerned with privacy and time alone. Indeed, fives tend to observe their experiences and then retreat into the safety of their own space and analyze what they feel. As a result of this preoccupation, they can be fairly talented at envisioning the "big picture" and running major organizations from the back room. Their primary passion is avarice in terms of their time and possessions, and their chief feature is withdrawal from experience.

Type 6 is the trooper

A person of this type is dynamically involved in many activities, all of which require proper reassurance from those around them. Troopers can be very loyal to the causes they support, so long as their self-doubt and trust issue are handled properly. Their primary passion is fear of everything, for which they keep a constant vigilance. The chief feature of a trooper is doubt that causes them to question everything in their lives over and over again.

Type 7 is the epicure

A person of this type is constantly on the lookout for fun and pleasure, and is always searching out positive possible alternatives. They like the good things in life and strive to stay optimistic. Bad results are often reframed into positive outcomes. Their primary passion is gluttony for the good life. Their chief feature is avoiding pain at all costs with lots of pleasant activities.

Type 8 is the boss

People of this type are dominated by the desire to control and be in charge. They tend to over-do everything in their lives, and as a result, the can often push peoples buttons. They like excess and all areas of life wealth, power, sex, food, drugs, and the like. On the positive side, the make excellent leaders and foster trust in other people to follow them. Their primary passion is lust for all things in life, not just sex! Their chief feature of the eight is its need to dominate and control situations.

Type 9 is the mediator

A person of this type can see all types of view but doesn't have one of his/her own. As a result, a nine will spend a lot of time doing meaningless tasks or spread out watching TV until all hours of the day or night. Indolence is their primary passion, which makes them indecisive and unwatchful of their own needs. Their chief feature is their self-forgetting nature.

Chapter 3: Type 1– The Reformer

The Type One Reformers are always on a mission to improve the world. They strive to overcome adversity. They are also known for being perfectionists. Ones are activists searching for acceptable reasoning for their missions of what they feel they must do to improve the world.

People who have Type One personality are meticulous and ethical. They have a strong sense of what is right and acceptable and what is wrong or unacceptable. Many Type One people become teachers, activists, and advocates for change. Their goal is to improve the world and people around them and avoid making any mistakes. They are orderly, well-organized, and can be demanding of the people around them. They try to maintain high standards which can cause them to be critical of others and come off as a perfectionist. They typically have problems with resentment and impatience. Type

Ones are discerning, noble, realistic, and wise at their best. They have high respect for moral standards and live up to those standards better than most people.

As a perfectionist, the possibility of being wrong is a tremendous concern and fear for a Type One personality. Their basic desire is to be balanced, have integrity, and an overall sense of doing what is good and right.

The most notable One personalities are those who have left behind comfortable lifestyles for the better good of others. They chase extraordinary adventures and do extraordinary accomplishments for the betterment of others. Even Type Ones on a lesser level still desire to be useful to others and to the environment.

On a more negative level, Type Ones are constantly justifying their actions to themselves and to others.

Ones are constantly beating themselves up for mistakes or wrongdoings.

If you are a Type One who is constantly listening to the unforgiving and nagging voice in your subconscious, learn to separate your self-worth from that voice. Instead, learn from the mistakes, accept that you cannot be perfect all the time and you will be able to use your inner voice for growth.

A Type One personality with a Nine-wing is more idealistic. They may use their ideas to justify their behavior. Their fear of being condemned by anyone turns them away from criticism. A Type One with a Two-wing becomes an advocate. They know the best ways to help others and improve their environment.

Stress Point

When Type Ones are stressed. They may show unhealthy level traits of Type Four personalities.

Some of these unhealthy traits may include:

Depression

Avoidance

Narcissism

Despair

Feelings of hopeless

Shame

Security Point

When Type Ones experience periods of growth, they may show average to healthy level traits of Type Seven personalities.

Some of these healthy traits may include:

Grateful

Appreciative

Joyous

Demonstrate goodness of life

Enthusiastic

Extroverted

Practical

Productive

Type 1 Levels of Development

Levels 1,2 and 3 are considered healthy levels of development. Remember that the traits exhibited in these levels can also be seen by Type Fours during their times of growth.

Levels 3, 4 and 5 are considered average levels of development.

Levels 6, 7 and 8 are considered unhealthy levels of development. Remember that the traits exhibited in these levels can also be seen by Type Sevens during times of stress.

Healthy:

Level 1

Extraordinary wisdom and discernment

They begin to understand what is actually realistic and know the best course of action to take in each situation.

Level 2

Reliable personal convictions

Their sense of right and wrong aligns with their religious and moral values. They desire to be reasonable, rational, self-disciplined, achieve balance and maturity in all things.

Level 3

High principles

They strive to be ethical, fair, and objective. Justice and truth are their primary values. Their sense of purpose, responsibility, and integrity help them teach others and witness to the truth.

Average:

Level 4

Idealist critics, crusaders, and advocates.

They are not satisfied with reality. It becomes their personal mission to improve everything. These are the people constantly serving multiple causes. They have a strong sense of how they feel things should be.

Level 5

Afraid of making mistakes

Everything must be consistent with their ideals. They are well-organized but impersonal and emotionally distant. They don't let their feelings or impulses show or control their actions in any way. They are workaholics, punctual, and demanding.

Level 6

Judgmental perfectionists

They are very opinionated about everything causing them to be highly critical of themselves and those around them. They constantly scold people who will never be able to live up to their standards of perfection. They can come across as abrasive and angry

Unhealthy:

Level 7

Dogmatic

They are inflexible, intolerant, and self-righteous. They believe they are the only one who can be right. They are strict in judgment but rationalize their own actions.

Level 8

Hypocritical

They obsess over the imperfections and mistakes of others, but they are blind to their own actions.

Level 9

Obsessive-compulsive disorder and depressive personality disorders are common mental health issues. They may experience severe depression or nervous breakdowns. They push others away to separate themselves from the imperfections of others.

Chapter 4: What Is Enneagram?

Enneagram is still a mystery to most people. While you're aware of the existence of different personality types everything else is an enigma. Sure, we come across different personality tests and quizzes online and in magazines, but they are usually incorrect. Remember, that type of content is only written for entertainment and it does not depict the true personality of an individual. Before you start the journey towards discovering your personality, it is important to understand the Enneagram and everything it entails.

Enneagram overview

The term Enneagram comes from Greek words ἐννέα (ennéa) meaning nine and γράμμα (gramma) referring to something that is drawn or written. So, what is it? Enneagram is not only the nine-pointed symbol but a powerful tool for both personal and collective transformation; it is a very specific system that organizes people into one of nine major personality types according to certain generalized diagnostic characteristics of their persona. What makes Enneagram so interesting is the fact individuals in any one of these personality types have many common characteristics along with prominent differences that set one type apart from the other. Each Enneagram personality type has a different pattern of feeling, acting, and thinking that stems from a deeper inner worldview or motivation.

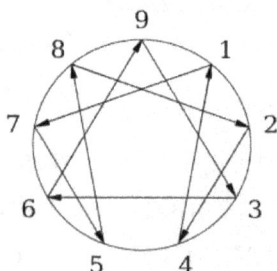

Figure 1: The Enneagram symbol (Photo credit: Wikimedia Commons)

Throughout the history, scholars, philosophers, and other scientists tried to categorize different types of personalities to explain people's behaviors. It is in human nature to try to understand and explain the way others act, feel, or think. A vast majority of personality categorizations also take into account parameters such as religion, gender, culture, and nationality. The Enneagram analysis transcends the ideas of gender and other parameters thus fostering a greater understanding of human psyche and personality through a universal language. What this type of analysis can teach us is that although every human being is unique and different, we do have many things in common. Both similarities to others and our own uniqueness define us and our perception of the world around us.

We can easily consider Enneagram as the map of consciousness underpinning all aspects of a person's life. Essentially, it gives a detailed insight into nine fundamentally different personality types, but it also elucidates nine ways of being in the world. Each personality type has their own attitudes toward different life aspects. As you'll get to see throughout this book, Enneagram is the key to understanding yourself and other people. Although it may seem like a complex method of self-development, Enneagram reveals the simplicity of life by making it easier to explain your and other individuals' actions, thoughts, and behaviors. Not only that, learning more about Enneagram and each personality type gives you a significant advantage in the competitive business world today.

Origins of the Enneagram

The Enneagram isn't a modern invention that helps us understand our own and someone else's personality. It has been here for many centuries which can only confirm the true significance of the personality model. The truth is that exact origin of the Enneagram is still a subject of many debates due to different accounts about its historical background and development because it evolved as an oral tradition. The earliest records of the Enneagram personality can be traced to the work of Evagrius Ponticus, a Christian monk, and ascetic who lived in Alexandria somewhere around the 4th century. Due to the trade with many cultures, at that time Alexandria was a place of diverse philosophical and spiritual traditions.

Ponticus identified eight deadly thoughts, logismoi, including gluttony and abstinence, fornication and chastity, avarice and freedom and from possessions, sadness and joy, anger and patience, acedia and perseverance, vainglory and freedom from vainglory, pride and humility, and jealousy and freedom from jealousy. The monk also wrote: "The first thought of all is that of the love of self; after this, the eight." Even though the presentation of the ninth deadly thought is inconsistent, it is impossible not to notice the parallel between ideas and Enneagram personality types.[1]

Furthermore, some variations of the Enneagram symbol was found in the geometry of Pythagoreans who were interested in the significance of numbers and their deeper meaning 4000 years ago. The idea that numbers have a greater meaning and the mysticism surrounding them was passed on through Plato as well as his disciple Plotinus and neo-Platonists. The Enneagram personality is also associated with the works of Philo of Alexandria, a Hellenistic Jewish philosopher. In his works, the tradition appears as the Tree of Life in the symbolism of ninefoldness linked with Cabalistic teachings. Moreover, Philo frequently engaged in numerology inspired by Pythagoreans and he strived to explain the meaning the religious importance of different numbers. While the Enneagram transcends religion, this information is still significant primarily because it demonstrates that roots of this personality analysis are everywhere.

The origins of Enneagram symbol can also be traced to the Muslim tradition or Sufi culture in Central Asia. The Islamic tradition is well-known for its major contributions to science and medicine. Sufis incorporated wisdom from previous traditions including Hindu, Jewish, Platonic, Pythagorean, Christian, Buddhist, Zoroastrian, and Taoist, but made sure the knowledge did not alter the idea of Oneness of God and the principle of unity. In the 14th century, the Naqshbandi Order of Sufism known as the Brotherhood of the Bees and Symbolists collected and preserved the Enneagram symbol.

In fact, it is assumed that a man who made the Enneagram known, George Ivanovich Gurdjieff Russian philosopher, encountered the tradition through Sufis when he visited the Sufi Sarmouni monastery in Afghanistan in the 1920s. He explored the method of understanding different personality types and published his teachings. The Russian philosopher used the Enneagram to elucidate the laws associated with the creation and unfolding of the universe and all its aspects and published his works in the 1930s. While G.I. Gurdjieff is credited for putting the spotlight on the Enneagram it is important to mention that he did not invent it nor he created personality types. A person who invented Enneagram personality theories is Oscar Ichazo, a Bolivian-born philosopher and a founder of Arica School (human potential movement group).Ichazo assigned personalities to each of the nine Enneagram positions and described different types of personalities, their inner emotions, concerns, and features in the 1960s.

In the early 1970s, a Chilean-born American-trained psychiatrist, Claudio Naranjo, gave an additional boost to the acknowledgment of the Enneagram personality in the Western culture. He extensively explored theories of personality and studied from Ichazo. His teachings at the Berkley influenced others to pay more attention to self-development based on the Enneagram personality types. Many other philosophers and psychiatrists adopted the Enneagram tradition and put more effort into exploring this important analysis of human character.

Chapter 5: How To Find Your Number

With The Enneagram

The power of the Enneagram to shed lights on the personality of a person cannot be underestimated. Through the exciting and thrilling guidance of the Enneagram, many people have discovered their personality traits, motivations and general outlook in life. This knowledge of "self" has granted them a much better understanding of who they are and why they behave the way they do.

The key to a happy life is to know yourself, accept yourself and then learn to deal with others. In fact, the more self-aware you are, the better you deal with others, which will contribute to your success in life. Michael Bloomberg once said, "You can only control three things: how hard you work, how honest you are and how well you deal with others."

Knowing and understanding your personality will greatly enhance your relationship with yourself and others. Having a strong, accurate and better knowledge of your personality enables you to deal

well with others. As Ian Morgan said, you are compassionate rather than judgmental and critical with people. You accept them just as they are, instead of trying to change them.

The Enneagram is a special tool that helps us to discover our personality types so we can better work on ourselves to become the best version of ourselves. It does not only show you your core personality traits, but also hidden / unconscious/subconscious fears, passions and virtues that drives your everyday life. Instead of being ruled by your unconscious temperamental and personality qualities, you gain control over them.

One of the amazing things about the Enneagram is that it exposes the hidden motivations behind people's actions. You see, sometimes it is not what someone does that is important, but rather the motivators behind their actions. You can look at a person's personality traits and behaviors, and still not understand the person. Yet, if you know the motive behind the person's action, you will be more likely to understand why the person acts in a certain way, and then deal well with the person.

How to Know Your Type of Enneagram

How do you know your Enneagram of Personality?

There are basically four ways to detect, recognize, and figure out your Enneagram of Personality:

Take an Enneagram Personality Typing test.

Attend an Enneagram discovery retreat with an Enneagram coach. Read Enneagram descriptions online or via a book and reflect.

Take an Enneagram Personality Typing Test:

The fastest way for you to discover your personality type is to take an Enneagram test. There are a lot of websites and apps out there offering free assessments services to help you determine your personality type. Free is not always the best. Therefore, you have to check reviews and read more about the website before you start using it. Meanwhile, there are credible websites also offering free Enneagram personality typing tests.

The key is to make sure you review the site before doing the test. You might be asked to pay a minimum of $10 for premium test assessment services. You have to make sure you analyze the site, read customer reviews and check their status before using the site. You can also consider using typing test apps which can also make the whole process easier for you.

Whether it is a website or an app, an Enneagram test is usually a typing system that automatically tells your personality by analyzing the input you entered into it. If you are the type that is prone to lying and hiding stuff, this is the time to be brutally honest with yourself. It is only through being open and honest that you can be able to input the right data which will be used to process your personality type.

Honesty is the key. You need to also avoid the delusive behavior of answering the questions based on how you wish to be, instead of who you are now. If you do that, the typing system will give you a wrong assessment about yourself. You need to answer the test questions based on how who you are currently. There will be several pages, it can vary from 10 to 14. Each page will have questions which might take less than 30 minutes to answer.

There are two main types of test questions: the classical Enneagram test, and the instinctual variant tests. The first one is the usual question-and-answer-type questions while the later involves rating character traits. Whichever way, avoid skipping questions so that you'll get an accurate assessment of your personality type.

Once you get the results, check your percentile scores to find the disposition of each quality traits inside you. Ideally, what you want to find out about your personality type and the other wing types. Many Enneagram coaches believe in the "two-wing" theory instead of just one wing.

So, consider looking at the wing personalities of the basic or core type. Share the results with trusted friends and family. Review the description of the character traits and find how your core and wing personality types play out in your life.

Attend an Enneagram Discovery Retreat with an Enneagram Coach

For some people, you just can't stay with a computer and internet connection to find your personality type. You might need the assistance of coach, a discussion group or a community to help you feel alive to the Enneagram personality typing.

Well, look for an Enneagram Personality Type retreats or live programs around. You can look for online or offline programs and then register. Through the retreat or workshop, your Enneagram coach will guide your coaching group to know what their personality types are.

You might be asked to answer a series of questions honestly and accurately, after which your personality type will be accessed by the coach through the answers provided. With this type of exercise, you'll not feel isolated. Your instructor will guide you and further helper you to explore areas about your personality that you have never thought about.

You should be careful about the kind of instructor you heed to. Before you choose an Enneatype event to attend, you should read carefully and know about the coach and instructor. You want to be sure that the instructor is skilled and has the track record for helping others to find their personality types.

Not only that, based on insights gleaned about your Enneatype, how you can start your personal development journey to start "masking" your vices and "unveiling" your virtues more and more. How can you develop your strengths and use them to advance your career, relationship, and social life? Check the program outline and have a full idea of what you will get before attending. This will help you avoid certain surprises.

Read Enneagram Descriptions Online or Via a Book and Reflect:

This is by far, the easier and the low-cost method to find your ideal personality type. When you choose to take a test, you might be asked to pay some amount of money. The same applies to attend a live or online event. However, you get value for money.

To find your personality type, just read the descriptions about each personality type over and over again. As you read them, you will notice that the descriptions will be exposing you to you. There will be a series of "Aha" moments which will cause you to explore your real type. It will be like an X-ray, running through your personality to expose hidden things that you were not aware of.

When it comes to your associated weaknesses or vices, you may tend to "feel exposed." Your hidden motives, fears, and desires that drive the things you do will be exposed. You might even "feel ashamed" of some of the things you do because you do them unintentionally. They are personality type actions that spring forth from your subconscious mind.

You will also feel strengthened by the knowledge of your strengths. The descriptions will shed light on the good part of you—your virtues or gifts. For example, as an achiever, you'll feel excited about your need to get things done and to succeed. This will make you accept yourself and be happy about who you are. In a sense, the personality typing exercise will help you to value yourself, improve yourself and develop high self-esteem.

Can Your Enneagram Type Change?

This is the question most people tend to ask after conducting a typing exercise.

Well, that is a good question. The fact is that your basic or core personality type remains fixed through your lifetime. It is your predisposed strategy for surviving and having your needs met in life. It is the basic lens through which you perceive, approach, and manage your life as a whole. You deeply rotted intentions and motives for doing things are gleaned from this Enneatype.

But here is the flip side, as you grow and pass through life; you get to learn many things. You acquire various experiences that improve your viewpoint and outlook in life. In a sense, it does not really change your basic Enneatype. What it does rather is to enhance your expression of the core traits of that Enneatype. Through the lessons, you acquire through life, you begin to adjust, improve, and grow.

In fact, self-discovery will lead to personal growth. Which means some of the vices or blind spots which are more visible now might be slightly masked through new subconscious programming. Your motives and drives for action might remain the same, but your character traits for expressing the notice will change. This might seem as though your core enneatype has blended with other types. Yet, that is far from the truth!

Here is another thing you have to be aware of. All the personality traits are already in your human soul. It is referred to as archetype. But what happens is that, through the life experiences, early programming and environmental influences on your personality, you will tend to be "burnt" towards one Enneatype than all others. Two or three personality types can also combine to run and govern a person's daily life.

Enneatype Combination

It is also important to know that your personality might be a triad. That means you might tend to connect with other Enneatypes which might not

be your core or dominant type. For example, you can have triads such as 8-9-1, 2-3-9.

Usually, people with Type One are also likely to be Type Nine. These two quality traits will combine to make them "thick". In addition to these two personality types, they might have Type One, Type Three, Type Nine or to mix up. The combination of Enneagram types in person to form a defining feature or quality of a person is known as "Tri-type".

You might want to ask yourself about the combination of Enneatypes that are operating in yourself. When you run your Enneatype test, you will observe the percentiles of your types in operation. The top three are what makes up your "Tri-type". You can notice how they subconsciously operate in your life by looking at your centers of intelligence.

Read through your descriptions of your personality combinations and then notice the motives, desires, fears, vices, and virtues related to each type and then reflect to see how they all operate in tandem inside you. This will enable you to understand how your Enneatype combination operates and how to work on yourself to improve your overall personality.

In some cases, you might also be seeing three Wing Types operating in your life. Take a closer look at them and try to rank them based on their strength level in you. The bottom line is that the Enneatype is not designed to put you in a box. You are a complex being and you might have a combination of features that make you unique, different, and outstanding.

Look for your basic type and then look for other combination types that go with it. Read through the description of the Enneatype over and over, and take a journal of things that resonated with you the most. What are some of the areas of your life that need working on? What must you reinforce in your life? Remember that the goal of the Enneagram is to help foster a good relationship with yourself and other people so that you can live a fulfilled life.

Chapter 6: Enneagram And Its History

As the old saying goes, everything that has a beginning has an end - and vise versa. Every process has a starting point, and every piece of history is felt in the future. This same situation extends to Enneagram. To fully understand what the term Enneagram means, we would have to go deep into its historical background and development. How did Enneagram begin? What led to its development? How was the idea of Enneagram conceived?

The word Enneagram is from two Greek words, ennea, which means "nine" and gramma meaning "written." The origin of Enneagram has been a notable controversy among scholars. The need arose because many people have found the personalities identified as being true to form even in their personal experiences. One of the earliest writings on the Enneagram, as opined by Palmer and Wiltse is found in the book of Evagrius Ponticus in the 4th century. In his book, Ponticus gave eight personalities, which he called logismoi meaning "deadly thoughts" with the critical thought as "love of self." This was created because Ponticus thought that whatever one does as a judgment of another person's trait is influenced by the personality of that person.

In other words, people with the 'challenger' personality will mostly take 'enthusiasm' as a negative trait simply because they don't exhibit it. To bolster this, Ponticus further says that;

"The first thought of all is that love of self (Philautia); after this [come] the eight."

These identifications given by Ponticus caused a lot of commotion as people wondered how true it was to equate love to personalities. How could love originate without being altered too? In response to that, Ponticus gave the "remedies" to the eight thoughts. These solutions will be used to answer whatever questions that has to do with or would erupt on the ideas. With these remedies, many people saw the need to adopt the thoughts of Ponticus with all carefulness. Whether the resources given to the eight thoughts are still relevant in today's world is debatable.

The eight thoughts didn't, however, get enough publicity. But with the works of G.I. Gurdjieff, the Enneagram was known everywhere. This could have been the origin of what Enneagram is, alongside its study today. It is pertinent to note that Gurdjieff still retained the eight thoughts from Ponticus. As a matter of fact, they served as the guiding tenets of his work.

In modern day, Oscar Ichazo, a Bolivian, could be said to be Enneagram originator. The nine personality studies in this contemporary age are from his lectures, most importantly, those that focus on ego-fixations, virtues, passions, and holy ideas, delivered by Oscar in the 1950s. Another report claims that Oscar's well-detailed self-development and orientation were actually how he started the teaching that begot Enneagram. The lessons on 'Proto-analysis' use the typical nine enneagram figures and ideas that are used today.

With the growth in awareness of Enneagram through Oscar's teaching, Africa institute based in Chile was established. However, it later moved to the United States of America when he relocated to South America. This is where the etymology of "Enneagram of Personality" can be traced to. Oscar later coined the term. As the enneagram personalities got enough establishments, Oscar needed to teach some of his students so that they would be able to take enneagram personalities around the globe and obviously to the next level.

In the 1970s, notable psychologists such as John Lilly and Claudio Naranjo went to

Oscar to learn about the concept of Enneagram. Little wonder why these two were part of the earliest students of Oscar to understand Enneagram of personality. The Chilean and psychiatrist, Claudio Naranjo (from Arica in Chile) was in Africa Institute to take a course. Naranjo, having learned a great deal from Oscar, decided to start his teachings on Enneagram in the United States.

He took the teaching with a differing view from what his teacher, Oscar, taught him. He influenced some priest, the Jesuit, who adopted it to spiritual dealings. Enneagram took another approach against what Oscar wanted. His different approach, though friendly and straightforward, was perceived by Oscar as shrewd and misunderstanding. Because of this, Oscar disowned Naranjo and labeled his teachings as treacherous even though his lessons with other teachers spread like wildfire in the 1970s. Because Naranjo was teaching his understanding of Enneagram, his theory grew very fast and had students too.

As the saying goes, 'you shall reap what you sow,' Naranjo also witnessed the same thing he did to his teacher as his students also misconstrued and betrayed him in the end. Naranjo taught different things which were taken for spiritual dealings, and his students taught things that seemed to be more business inclined. Instead of preaching their teacher's teachings, they focus on a paradigm shift which saw them exploring the business side of Enneagram.

In the 1980s and 1990s, diverse authors such as Helen Palmer, Richard Rohr, Elizabeth Wagele and Don Richard Riso, started various publications on Enneagram. Meanwhile, the theories they taught and published are a mixture of how Enneagram erupted. In today's enneagram theories, attention to what the context of their application is, solely determined their usage and understanding. As part of the publishers, this book takes no particular view other than simplifying everything concerning Enneagram.

Maybe because enneagram founders understood and taught Enneagram at a different situation, many of Enneagram theories are basically on spirituality and business —as noted in the introduction. In fact, today, many authors would love to equate Enneagram to spirituality. This is very wrong, considering the history of the Enneagram. The account given here was confirmed from different authors and looking at it from different opinions. Enneagram is used in psychology and even neuroscience today. A lot of attention has been drawn to it because of how people have known about it lately.

Know that the historical background of Enneagram follows an intricate pattern. From one scholar to another, from one philosopher to another, and from one teacher to another, the Enneagram concept had followed a fantastic design which had led to its rapid development over the past century. Additionally, the idea is still being transformed and developed with new ideas coming from young minds. Now, our next chapter will focus on where the concept of Enneagram was developed.

Where Enneagram was developed

The exact nature of where Enneagram originated has been a mirage since its inception in the 4th century. As noted from the beginning of this book, contextual understanding of Enneagram has been developed through various conceptions and teachings from scholars with diverse ideas. Many people who published works to influence others on the nature of Enneagram never had the intention of the deduced meanings. Interestingly, one of the concepts of psychology that have suffered a lot of false conceptions is Enneagram.

Many people that start Enneagram do so with what could be considered diluted knowledge regarding where it was initially developed. Different conceptions of Enneagram have contributed immensely to what we know it as today. Here, the 'places' where Enneagram was developed are the most prominent ones throughout its history. They are where Enneagram can best be understood and found. They are the teachings of the notable more profound of the Enneagram personalities.

Since Enneagram has entertained different approaches and alarming concern from different professions –such as psychology, neurology, theology, and lots more –the need to understand where it was developed rose to some degree. It is pertinent to note that where Enneagram of personality developed from, as discussed here, is based on the diverse scholars of the Enneagram and not that there is a concrete building like a pyramid of Egypt or a monument center that begat it.

Additionally, Enneagrams development is based on the fact that there are different schools of thoughts with different terminologies. As well as approaches, conception, overlapping and merging, teachings, dealings, etc. The Enneagram we have today, though quite different from its original intention, is gotten from the places it evolved.

In past studies, psychologists have identified six basic 'places' where Enneagram originated. Keep in mind that this is different from the history of the Enneagram. The origins and places where it was developed to simplify the teachings of the developers. Below are the six 'places' where Enneagram was developed:

Don Richard Riso

Don Richard Riso is a neurotic approach to the study of the Enneagram. Its manner of dealing is to give a full description of the sequence in the nine personalities from the neurotic approach through to normal development and then to healthy emotion. The development of this kind of Enneagram was based on giving an analysis of how emotional health has evolved using the neurons in the body. Based on this approach and development, there have been many beliefs and teachings on this kind of Enneagram personality. It contributes to where the enneagram personality was developed.

Oscar Ichazo development of enneagram personalities

An approach that is based on Ichazo was developed in order to give the application of the nine personalities using varying schemata like ego and fixations in order to provide an analysis of self-development. Many books have used this approach where enneagram personalities had been developed both in the application and in actual teachings. The goal of the Enneagram in this approach is to provide the schema in self-development using the fixations theories.

Hameed A. Ali (A. S. Almaas) development of Enneagram personalities

Hameed A. Ali's development of Enneagram personalities is a psychological approach which evolved as another different kind of Enneagram. With this approach, Enneagram of personality is only a combination of studies from disciplines in the therapy of Gestalt through to that of Zen and the Reichian. It is purely psychological, thus studies the mind as well as how they affect human behavior. This particular type of Enneagram is probably the type that had received the most publications and teachings.

Claudio Naranjo development of enneagram personalities

Being a psychiatrist, Claudio proposed an approach that substitutes and replaces the usage of neurotic terms and strategies with psychiatric jargons and dealings. The total reliance on neurotic usage of transactions as a determinant of Enneagram personality was denounced and changed. Essentially, everything boiled down to the psychiatric approach. Well, because this approach is more or less synonymous to the disorder of humans and this is why many people reject it for a better approach – meanwhile only those within the field love to use it. Whenever you read a book relating to Enneagram that utilizes this kind of personality developed, adjust your attention to their terminologies only.

Helen Palmer

Helen Palmer is the sort of Enneagram that focuses on the overall narrative of prevalent teachings. Just like this book, this development is in learning the general idea as there is no particular niche given. On a closing note, this Enneagram developed here is based on the teachings and approaches it had from its inception. It is not to nullify that Enneagram is based on the nine human personalities in their social relations and reactions to things and people. Based on this general background, it is believed that the development of Enneagram is from the first developer.

Oscar Ichazo development of Enneagram personalities

The Oscar Ichazo development is an approach that was developed as a way to give the application of the nine personalities, through the use of varying schemata, ego, for example. Psychologists and other great developers of Enneagram have agreed, at least to some extent, that those enneagram personalities had been in man since childbirth. Noting that there were not many new insights found when they traced the origin of the Enneagram to inhuman sources. In fact, the only thing that was discovered was the naming, description, and teachings of the nine Enneagram personalities which have been believed to be an influence of different developers explained at the beginning of this chapter. The line of enneagram development is evolving, and the probability of having much more approaches in the future is very high.

Lastly, note that the development of Enneagram has followed several approaches; however, none has ruled out the context of birth in the perception of the concept by the developer. This is one of the reasons enneagram personalities have many misconceptions even from the onset. The approach given here is the underlying factor which proves that Enneagram is a model and also a system of nine human personalities, using the names mostly adopted and not the popularly known misconception because this book will give you a complete introduction to the Enneagram personalities.

This chapter should familiarize you with the knowledge of the different school of thoughts in regards to the Enneagram. Having a deep understanding of where the concept originated from would also go a long way in putting you through a straight path concerning this journey. This chapter will help broaden your horizon as regards this concept. Now, which Enneagram school do you fancy? Which do you find appealing? Once you lay this foundation, the rest will fall into place.

Chapter 7: Organizational Astrology

Say again if you don't say astrology and business blend. Kings, leaders, and other powerful figures have used astrology throughout the centuries to guide important political and financial decisions."Millionaires don't use astrologers," Morgan famously said. "Those were known to consult his famous astrologer Evangeline Adams on both his business and his personal lives.

So how can astrology in the modern era be helpful to companies? Today, astrologers consult record labels, production companies, and hedge funds. The modern astrologers continue an old tradition of offering advice and counsel based on their understanding of natural cycles and the relationships of these cycles to our personal and working lives, ranging from everything from the timing of record releases to the best new hires.

Like the use of the Enneagram, astrology can also contribute to the detection and isolation of characteristic characteristics in people that lead to a better understanding of how and why they function. The astrological diagram shows the potential of an entity, an event, or an organization and also particular characteristics and trends evolving over time.

In my own practice working with companies and organizations, the charts of new and prospective workers are analyzed, seminars are performed on retreats, and interaction models among employees are assessed on the basis of their astrological charts.

As I explain my services to new clients, it is often necessary to teach how and when astrology can be useful, and explain the difference between astrology with "sun signs" and more extensively astrological studies that I use in my practice.

Most of us know the "star side" astrology. On the basis of the symbol, on the day you were born, your sun is identified certain characteristics and qualities associated with that sign. Horoscopes and books on sun signs exist and can either be remarkably accurate or completely off-base, depending on their reliability.

But saying that astrology with sun signs encompasses the art of astrology means that, every day, watching the sun tells you all about astronomy. This lacks a vast body of information which can literally be applied not only to the business world but also to life in general.

Apart from sunshine, there are traditionally nine other astrological planets: Moon, Mercury, Venus, Mars, Jupiter, Saturn, Uranus, Neptune, and Pluto. Many astrologers also deal with the asteroids, Chiron is the most common, but other asteroids can also provide useful information. The sign which rose on the horizon when you were born (or an event or company) is called the "rising sign," which is also taken into consideration when you draw a chart.

Each planet or asteroid represents a different life, value, gift, or challenge. The rising sign demonstrates how we approach life, how we show others, and how others understand us most easily during a first encounter.

When examining the charts for work-related questions, I typically analyze the location of planet Mercury first. Mercury governs or controls the contact domain. Write, speak, listen, learn, teach. You name it if it is related to communicating orally, in writing, sung or signed, you can bet that Mercury is involved.

As in most relationships, conflicts at work often focus on communication issues. By looking at the sign that Mercury is in, immediate details about the style of communication can be gained. For example, Mercury in Aries would be frank, optimistic, and impatient. Cancer Mercury is imaginative; it has a feeling and incredible memory. Combine the two in a working environment and look either to constant conflict or to exploit some of the tension and energy that can lead to strife and to create something new and untested.

An astrologer can clarify and identify the unique qualities of each Mercury sign and help to find ways to connect and engage different signs in positive rather than challenging ways.

I had many valuable tactical sessions just because I led groups to discuss the sign and house of the Mercury of each person and how their style of interaction helped or hindered the work of the entire group.

Astrology is also a tool for what I like to call "sage time," apart from using the chart to solve the personality dynamism of the workplace. Just as our forefathers, and many modern farmers, used moon and star cycles to decide on the best time for planting, weeding, and harvesting, astrology will lead us to launch new ventures and proposals at the right time.

Through looking at the current earth cycles, it is possible to determine and prepare for the daily, weekly, and monthly planetary conditions. Traditionally the new moon is a good time to plant the seeds of a project, and the full moon is time to see both faults and benefits, while the decreasing moon is the time to harvest and reduce all harvests.

When we apply nature cycles to our work in the world, we become more harmonious with the natural flow of life. Astrology offers another tool for closer integration of the rhythm and pattern of the natural world into our everyday lives and for creating a unique partnership between man and nature, which is now more necessary than ever.

Although it may seem unusual for some to combine the astrology and business worlds, previous experience indicates that this marriage has significance and provides potentially infinite opportunities for new development and understanding. Through building on the lessons of the past, we will build new models for a better future.

Self-Knowledge - Does it Give You a Better Life?

What are your ideas?

The Enneagram is a really accurate and natural method of observation. It can be used with incredible accuracy to define nine basic types of personalities or operating styles, which illustrate the basic characteristics in a variety of ways. These core types define how the main characteristics of the individual inhibit their choices, lives, and connections with what we call their essence or their true nature.

In its most basic sense, it is an analysis of the nine principal personality types, which demonstrates that each type shifts between two different types in its most fluid form under different circumstances and typically is colored by the type or the point adjacent to the diagram. This triangulated personality version is also known as "The Law of Three." When we become conscious of our basic operating type, we can answer questions like · When is it good to give up on our emotions, and when is it better to observe them from a distance?

• When does it cost, or is it easier to stay in a relationship?

• When is it good to stay with something, and when is it prudent to look for new possibilities?

• When is it prudent to work with the mind, and when are we going to give in to our sentiments?

• Is it prudent to evaluate something too much, or is it more effective to simply decide and do something?

• When is hedonism better, and when is the intimacy better? Could we blend these two?

• In what situations should we be blunt and back down when?

• At what point are we to look at a new future, and when are we to continue and improve our position?

• When are we to find a further physical activity, and when are we to look for mental or creative stimulation? Is there a struggle?

• Can we have a peaceful coexistence of security and spontaneity in our lives?

• If we don't like our jobs, will we lead our existing life?

• When is the time to stop for a long time?

• When is it necessary and when is it overdue?

It will help if we are willing to look at the more hidden aspects of our personalities; otherwise, it will be impossible to unravel our hidden potential. Most of us want to take a spiral of change from point A to point B. It's an attractive idea, but not very effective.

Below are some of the key features represented by this program. One sure way to learn what features hold us back is to ask our friends, colleagues, and family who are usually all too happy to show us some of our less appealing characteristics.

There are different perspectives to decide the predominant kind, and I will list underneath nine questions that clearly concern the nine kinds, and in this order:

1. You have an endless stream of judgmental feelings and compare yourself to others constantly.

2. You are socially optimistic and drawn to strong people and offer them assistance to defend them.

3. It is important that you provide others with a picture of achievement, no matter how you feel inside.

4. You are impatient of ordinary life, fascinated by the exceptional, dramatic, and tragic.

5. You appear to be silent and invisible at events, rather than communicating or participating.

6. You are very aware of your own feelings and other people's feelings and suspect of people's secret motives towards you.

7. You tend to avoid deep emotional contact, to prefer fun activities, to talk pleasantly, and to do many things at once.

8. You love being strong and never allowing people to profit from you and admire such qualities in others.

9. You find it hard to keep a personal point of view, but you can easily recognize and support others ' positions. What we are trying to achieve in this way is to really use the mirror of our relationships in order to clarify who we are and why we operate in ways that are destructive or harmful for others and for ourselves.

If we can constructively observe our habits and qualities and it will be easier to watch them disappear without judging them. The more we fight a habit, the easier it will be to let go. Ask any smoker. Tell any smoker! Worse still, through compulsion, it is acquiring bad habits and not learning, as this forces only that habit down, and another one emerges easily. That truth is well known to anyone who has actually tried to give up any addiction or obligation that they believe is no longer useful to them. It is also understood among behavior therapists who deal with addictions.

You might call the principal characteristics of each form of addiction, something like that, but the good news is that they lose their power over us by watching them embrace. When we begin to lose sight of these so-called negative traits, we find a quite obvious change in our relationships with others and ourselves.

A new survey was conducted in the United States of 733 million people on the reasons for their popularity. The top five responses were honest to all, well-disciplined, good relationships, supportive spouses, and working harder than others.

Many of these qualities are some of the virtues of certain forms, and insight helps to gain a greater understanding of your strengths and limitations, so possibilities and creative solutions become easier to see.

The Enneagram - Coaching in Troubling Times

The Enneagram in Coaching

What if people had spent hundreds of years considering the motivational patterns outside people's consciousness, supporting their choices? The Enneagram is a system with deep roots developed over many years and contexts. It's more than a personality typing exercise: it's a way to identify key motivation and attitude patterns so you can improve the task.

As a coach, you help customers change. Some of these changes are more difficult to sustain. In a similar situation, the Enneagram is a way to think about which changes work and why the changing pattern that works for a particular customer can have different results for a client. For different reasons, people can follow the same behavior patterns. The better your tools for identifying driving motivations, the better your chances of producing positive and sustainable change.

Learning about the Enneagram has the same benefits that other learning brings you deeper into the human state. It allows you to recognize some of your own unconscious decisions and to understand better the impact you have on others. The Enneagram even has spiritual dimensions for some people. There are more specific reasons for coaches to add the Enneagram to their customers ' tools and perspectives.

The coaches who study the Enneagram will be in a position to: discover the advantages of certain behaviors because they know better than they can hold the same benefits. Maintain an understanding of the whole person when manipulating other attitudes or behaviors.

Have you ever coached a client who at least appeared to be two different people? The Enneagram provides a unique perspective on how people under different conditions move to different styles of personality. It is a dynamic model that reveals the nature of our relationships with ourselves and other people. If you've ever asked, "Was that me?" or had coached both Dr. Jekyll and Mr. Hyde, then you're deeply interested in the template the Enneagram has to offer.

Perhaps most importantly, the Enneagram acknowledges that our greatest strength can also become our most vulnerable sector (and our challenges can hold the key to new opportunities). It makes us conscious that we have to live with all our qualities. We can't just get rid of the characteristics; we have to reframe them to work for us. The use of the Enneagram helps coaches and their customers tolerate a variety of features and to isolate points of possible and desirable change.

Whether you're a full-time trainer or a coach of your team, you know that your coaches are influenced by their culture. This culture is sometimes toxic. Every news agency broadcasts an imminent disaster; the economy is threatening jobs and housing; the poor air quality or the latter bug is scaring people. Once you encounter them, you put all these challenges to the table.

Troublesome people must be rescued from the swift sand by someone based on solid soil. Which means you have to be able to panic without crying. It means you have to recognize fear without being caught up in it. It means that you must be able to reach a customer and then remain close. You must catch them before they sink.

An Enneagram is an excellent tool to meet a customer and to establish a strong, versatile link. It is a framework that explains the usual reasons and tactics and how they under stress are modified. Within the Enneagram, one of nine core patterns is recognized in itself. You understand that their way of behaving is more formal than they know and that adjusting their meaning of signature actions will alter what they say. We realize that the past does not build a destiny and that no performance style is so strong that it can not ultimately become a liability.

As a coach, the Enneagram can be used in two ways. Second, it allows you to stay grounded and to develop a fast, deep connection to use the coaching session best. Using Enneagram types as a template, a working hypothesis is quickly developed that drives the attitudes and behaviors of your clients. If it feels' like you can read my mind,' you can very quickly create a warm, meaningful relationship.

The Enneagram is a dynamic system describing the movement and change of people. This means you're not "true" or "wrong" about an Enneagram type; you've just taken up actions that might lead to a constituency of similar patterns. It offers you the first step in working together to improve or alter its appraisal when the customer transitions to a different pattern. If you provide perspectives that exactly match your client, you build relationships. If you switch from something that is almost right to something that is truer, customers feel like you move with them, and that also deepens their relationship.

You can also use the Enneagram to help the consumers become aware of their characteristics. You encourage your clients to establish new connections between old behaviors and attitudes, as you explain Enneagram patterns. You see yourself differently, and you have a new map to explore the less developed parts of your personalities. Through the Enneagram, they develop a new sense of strength to meet troubled times.

The Enneagram describes remarkably flexibly and accurately how people change and develop as a result of their experience. This fits well with the subconscious information coaches who already have what works for their clients. This makes learning quick and implemented as it is taught. Training with real people gives you real-time opportunities to incorporate the mentioned trends and improvements. It makes it easy for you to interact with the Enneagram. You can learn how you can strengthen relations when going through different theories.

Whilst spending many, many hours learning the Enneagram, you can also take as little as two days of training, and use it to gain immediate feedback and insight into your coaching conversations. You will also note that the Enneagram learning provides invaluable help for preserving your own strengths during trouble-free times.

Chapter 8: The Challenger Subtypes

The three subtypes associated with the challenger are satisfaction, possession, and solidarity. You can learn more about these subtypes and what they mean below.

Self-Preservation: Satisfaction

Challengers have a tendency to be extremely confident. Their personality type is strong, productive, and direct. They are known as powerful and effective individuals. They have a strong survivor instinct and regularly take on the role of a guardian for many others, often being seen as a motherly or fatherly figure to those in their lives.

The downside to this strong tendency in the challenger type is that they can quickly become frustrated or intolerant if their needs are not being met. Because they are typically so good at meeting their own needs, this can create a feeling of distress or internal chaos in the challenger. When they do reach this state of intolerance, they can become very direct in their approach of having their needs met. They're known to be unapologetic and to show no remorse for the tactics they use to get their needs met.

One-on-One: Possession

When a challenger is dominant in the subtype of possession, they have a tendency to break rules and become rebellious. They may even become a trail blazer. These individuals can be impulsive and intense, with a strong desire to create change. The actions they take in creating this change are often rooted in an unapologetic nature. Challengers are nearly always willing to disrupt others and the system in order to gain power and influence, which they then use to make change. A challenger who is in this position strongly desires serving for a worthy cause, though they rarely want to do so from a "standby" position. They would rather be in charge or playing a highly central role in making it happen.

If a challenger is out of balance with their subtype of possession, they are likely to become excessively challenging toward the "system." This can result in chaos or destruction, as not every system was made to be disrupted. They may become restless and frustrated, and their powerful and confident nature may become obsessive and slightly aggressive as they push too hard to be in control.

Social: Solidarity

When the challenger is in balance and in a place of service, they may be dominant in the subtype of solidarity. They can be fiercely loyal to people or causes, often going out of their way to have the needs of the other person or cause met. They exercise the same confidence and power that they use to have their own needs met and use this as a means to get the needs of the others met, too.

The challenger tends to be highly sensitive towards injustice and will fight for fairness for all. They dislike unfair social norms and will use their disruptive tendency to shake things up and create chaos if need be, as a means to help them balance things back into a just fashion. Although the challenger prefers to refrain from being in a vulnerable position, they will invite tough feedback from close allies. In fact, they appreciate these types of feedback because it encourages them to do better.

Chapter 9: Introducing The Nine Types

Identifying your type marks the beginning of your work with the Enneagram; this also fuels your understanding of its dominant issues. Although we still recognize in ourselves behaviors of all of the nine types, our most determining traits are grounded on any of the types. If you follow the expositions closely, you should be able to discover your type with a high degree.

For the time being, think and feel the following type names and brief descriptions to see which two or three strikes you as an individual or relate to your personality. Keep in mind that the characteristics allow me to share merely a couple of highlights and never represent the entirety of each individual personality type.

Type One: The Reformer.

The principled, idealistic type. ONES are generally honest and diligent, accompanied by a strong sense of ideal as well as inappropriate. These are typically teachers and crusaders, always striving to enhance things but scared of making an error. Well-organized, orderly, and fastidious, they make an effort to maintain high standards but can slip into being critical and perfectionistic. They have struggles with repressed temper and irritability. At their full capacity, healthy ONES are clever, discreet, practical, and virtuous, in addition to being morally heroic.

Type Two: The Helper.

The caring, interpersonal type. TWOS are empathetic, sincere, and warm-hearted. These are generally friendly, generous, and self-sacrificing; however, they can become emotional, flattering, and people-pleasing. These are motivated to be in close proximity to other people, and these types of people often do things for others to be needed. They generally have problems looking after themselves and acknowledging their personal needs. In their best state, healthy TWOS are unselfish and kind and have unconditional love for themselves as well as others.

Type Three: The Achiever.

The adaptable, success-oriented type. THREES are self-assured, attractive, and charming. They are ambitious, competent, and energetic, and they tend to be status-conscious and highly driven for personal advancement. THREES in many cases, tend to be worried about their reputation and just what people opine of them. They usually have issues with workaholism and competitiveness. At their very best, healthy THREES are self-accepting, reliable, and the whole lot. They tend to be — role models who motivate other people.

Type Four: The Individualist.

The romantic, introspective type. FOURS are self-conscious, sensible, reserved, and calm. The FOURS are known as self-revealing, emotionally honest, and personal, but they can also be moody and self-conscious. They feel vulnerable and defective; as a result, they withhold themselves from others. They usually have issues with self-indulgence and self-pity. At their very best, healthy FOURS are determined and highly innovative, inclined to renew independently and improve their own experiences.

Type Five: The Investigator.

The intense, cerebral type. FIVES are aware, perceptive, and inquisitive. They are known for their ability to concentrate and focus on developing complex ideas and skills. Always independent and innovative, they can become preoccupied with their thoughts and imaginary constructs. They become detached, yet high-strung and intense. They have difficulties with isolation, eccentricity, and nihilism. In their finest state, healthy FIVES are generally visionary leaders, frequently ahead of their time and in a position to see the world in an utterly new way.

Type Six: The Loyalist.

The committed, security-oriented type. SIXES are dependable, industrious, and trustworthy, but they can also be defensive, equivocal, and highly nervous — running on stress while moaning about it. They are commonly vigilant and hesitant but can also be sensitive and rebellious. These types of people usually have difficulty with self-doubt and mistrust. At their best, healthy SIXES are internally steady, self-assured, and self-dependent, fearlessly supporting the poor and feeble.

Type Seven: The Enthusiast.

The busy, productive type. SEVENS are all-around, positive, and impulsive. Playful, high-boisterous, and practical, these types of people can also be over-extended, scattered, and undisciplined. These types of people continually see new and interesting experiences; however, they can end up distracted and fatigued by staying on the go. They usually have difficulty with superficiality and thoughtfulness. In their finest form, healthy SEVENS focus their talents on worthwhile goals, becoming joyous, highly accomplished, and full of gratitude.

Type Eight: The Challenger.

The powerful, dominating type. EIGHTS are self-confident, strong, and assertive. We see them as protective, resourceful, and decisive. They can also be proud and domineering. This type feel that they must control their environment, often becoming confrontational and intimidating. They lack interpersonal relationship skills. At their best, healthy EIGHTS are self-mastering— they use their strength to improve others' lives, becoming heroic, magnanimous, and sometimes historically great.

Type Nine: The Peacemaker.

The easygoing, self-effacing type. NINES are accepting, trusting, and stable. They are good-natured, kindhearted, tolerant, and loyal, but can also be too prepared to go along with people to maintain the tranquility. They desire everything to generally be without dispute but can tend to be self-satisfied and minimize anything disturbing. They ordinarily have difficulty with passivity and doggedness. In their finest form, healthy NINES are indomitable and all-embracing; they are able to bring people together and heal conflicts.

Things to Keep in Mind About Type

We all have a small combination of types within our general personality; a definite pattern or design is our "home base," so we return to it over and over again. Our foundational type stays the same throughout life. Even though people change and develop in numerous ways, they do not change from one basic personality type to another. Please note that:

• Our personality types description applies to males and females and are universal in effect. Definitely, men and women might exhibit a similar mindsets, traits, and inclinations somewhat in different ways, but the fundamental issues of the type remain precisely the same.

• Know that not everything in the description of your basic type will apply to you all the time. This stems from the belief that most of us vacillate always among the healthy, average, and unhealthy features that constitute our personality type, as we'll see during our discussion of the Levels of Development (Chapter 5). While we read along, we'll find that growing maturation or increasing concerns have a tremendous influence on how we are revealing our type.

• Even though we have provided each type a comprehensive identity (such as the Reformer, the Helper, and so forth), in exercise we would like to use its Enneagram number. Numbers tend to be value neutral — they provide an honest, shorthand way of talking about the type. Besides what is claimed, the denotative ranking of the types is not relevant: being a type with a bigger number is not superior to being a type with a lesser number. For instance, it is not more beneficial to be a NINE compared to a ONE.

• Not one of the personality types is superior or inferior than any other — all types possess distinctive assets and liabilities, strengths and deficiencies. Some types can be more appreciated than others in a given community or group. Nevertheless, you will soon discover more concerning many of the types, you will notice that nearly as each has distinctive abilities; they all have varied constraints.

• Whichever type you are, you have all nine types in you, to some degree. To examine them all and see them all functioning in you is to see the full spectrum of human nature. This consciousness provides you much more understanding of and empathy for others, because you'll know many areas of their unique habits and responses in yourself. It will be much more complicated to condemn the aggressiveness of EIGHTS or the masked deprivation of TWOS, for example, if we are mindful of aggressiveness and neediness within ourselves. If you examine all nine types personally, you will realize how interdependent they might be — similarly as the Enneagram sign signifies all of them.

Typing Others

We really feel strongly that it is always more frustrating to utilize the Enneagram to type other people compared to its use on ourselves. Everyone shows blind spots, and there are various likely differences among the types that it is unavoidable that we simply will not be acquainted with all of them. Mainly because of our own individual prejudices, it is very likely that we have an outright aversion to some types.

Keep in mind that the Enneagram needs to be used mainly for self-discovery and self-understanding. Additionally, identifying our type or that of someone else, can give us with many valuable ideas, nevertheless, it cannot begin to tell us every little thing about the individual, any more than knowing a person's race or nationality will.

In themselves, a type informs us nothing about the person's certain background, cleverness, talent, integrity, personality, or many other factors. On the other hand, our type really does tell us a great deal about the way we experience the world, the blends of options we are likely to have, the standards we maintain, what inspires us, how we respond to people, how we react to stress, and lots of other fundamental things. As we become acquainted with the personality models presented by this method, we more effortlessly value perspectives that are different from our very own.

The Deeper Purpose of The Enneagram

Distinguishing oneself as one of nine personality types can be inspiring. Initially in our lives, we possibly may see the pattern and general principle for the way we have lived and behaved. At a particular point, nonetheless, "determining our type" becomes enclosed into our self-image and may really continue to block the way of our continual development.

Certainly, some students of the Enneagram have turned out to be connected to their personality type —"Of course I get frenzied! Besides, I'm a SIX," or "You realize how we SEVENS are! We simply have to stay on the go!" Justifying debatable habit or adopting a more rigid personality are misuses of the Enneagram. However, by enabling us to learn how jammed we're in our trances as well as how estranged we're from our essential nature, the Enneagram encourages us to search deeply into the puzzle of our real identity.

It's designed to present a process of inquiry which will lead us to a deeper truth concerning ourselves and our place on the planet. Nonetheless, we make use of the Enneagram basically to arrive at a much better self-image, we'll stop the process of discovering (or, actually, recovering) our real character. While understanding our type offers us significant information, that information is largely an embarkation point for a much greater journey.

To sum up, knowing our type is not the final destination. The goal of this work is to stop the automatic reactions of the personality by bringing awareness to it; exclusively by providing insight and transparency to the elements of personality we can awaken—which is why I have written this book.

Chapter 10: The Achiever

You have a passion for being successful at whatever you do. Your purpose is to encourage colleagues, friends, and families on their life journey. You are an excellent mentor who enjoys making a difference in the world.

It is easy for you to forget who you are. You get so caught up in being whatever you need to be to be successful that you ignore the real you. If you are going to find your passion and purpose you need to be who you are. You need to risk being vulnerable.

At your best, you are a caring mover and shaker in the world. You bring energy and compassion to whatever you do. You also have a natural desire and passion to mentor those you care about helping to bring out the best in themselves.

People of this personality type need to be validated in order to feel worthy; they pursue success and want to be admired. They are frequently hard working, competitive and are highly focused in the pursuit of their goals, whether their goal is to be the most successful salesman in the company or the "sexiest" woman in their social circle. They are often "self-made" and usually find some area in which they can excel and thus find the external approbation which they so desperately need. Threes are socially competent, often extroverted, and sometimes charismatic. They know how to present themselves, are self-confident, practical, and driven. Threes have a lot of energy and often seem to embody a kind of zest for life that others find contagious. They are good networkers who know how to rise through the ranks. But, while Threes do tend to succeed in whatever realm they focus their energies, they are often secretly afraid of being or becoming "losers."

Threes can sometimes find intimacy difficult. Their need to be validated for their image often hides a deep sense of shame about who they really are, a shame they unconsciously fear will be unmasked if another gets too close. Threes are often generous and likable, but are difficult to really know. When unhealthy, their narcissism takes an ugly turn and they can become cold blooded and ruthless in the pursuit of their goals.

Because it is central to the type three fixations to require external validation, Threes often, consciously and unconsciously, attempt to embody the image of success that is promoted by their culture. Threes get in trouble when they confuse true happiness, which depends on inner states, with the image of happiness which society has promoted. If a Three has a "good" job and an "attractive" mate, she might be willing, through an act of self-deception which is also self-betrayal, to ignore the inner promptings which tell her that neither her job, nor her mate are fulfilling her deeper needs. Even the most "successful" Threes, who generally appear quite happy, often hide a deeply felt sense of meaninglessness. The attainment of the image never quite satisfies.

Threes can sometimes mistype themselves when they mistake the more superficial features of their personalities as indicators of their type. So, for instance, an intellectual Three might mistype as a Five; a Three who is devoted to her role as mother might think she is a Two; a Three in a leadership position might mistype as an Eight and so on. Regardless of the manifestation however, the core of the type Three fixation is the deep need for external validation.

American business is a particularly strong Three culture where performers get a lot of positive reinforcement for being productive and efficient. A danger for

Threes is concentrating on external praise or material rewards while losing contact with who they are inside. It's difficult for them to step out of their roles, feel their own feelings, and decide for themselves what is important.

Strengths: Successful, energetic, high achiever

Problems: Over worked, impatient, competitive

Speaking style: Enthusiastic, motivating themselves and others for success

Lower emotional habit: Vanity, based on keeping up a good image and always being successful

Higher emotion: Truthfulness, which is the willingness to go beyond appearances and develop personal authenticity

Archetypal challenge: To let go of image and social persona and find one's inner essence

Psychological defenses: Threes use the defense mechanism of identification to avoid failure and maintain a self-image of being "successful." (Identification is a kind of pervasive role-playing and losing oneself in image).

Somatic patterns: As feeling types who put everything into productivity and results, Threes can accrue a lot of tension around their chest and heart. They are the original "Type A's" and need to watch out for early heart attacks or a weakened immune system. Underneath a strong layer of chest tension, there is usually deep sadness from loss of contact with the inner self.

Core Belief: the world values winners, so I must avoid failure at all cost.

With this core belief, the Three's focus of attention is on whether they are winning or losing, achieving or failing. Being valued and recognized for their achievements is a strong driver for Threes. This operates below the level of conscious awareness and underlies everything that they do.

With their focus on winning and achieving, Threes have an optimistic outlook to life. They are confident people who believe in themselves and their abilities. Threes can be charming people, who can change their image to suit the environment they are in. This chameleon-like nature helps them get on in any environment enabling them to succeed wherever they go. Threes are industrious by nature. They work hard and long hours, and you will often find them taking their work home with them, unable to switch off their drive to succeed.

Because winning is everything, they value themselves and others on the level of their achievements. They will proudly display their trophies and symbols of success.

Whilst Threes are the core point of the Heart Triad, the center for feelings, they are also the most out of touch with their own feelings of all the Heart Triad types. They are so busy striving to achieve that they do not have time for feelings and for self-reflection. In fact, time is money and to be used wisely. They can be very protective of their time and will not allow anyone to waste it.

At their best, you will often find Threes at or near the top of successful organizations.

In sport, you will find them as charming winners who will bask in the spotlight, enjoying the respect they have earned through their achievement. But not for long - Threes are only as good as their last triumph, and will be on to achieving their next victory!

Their strong drive to achieve creates the Threes blind spot, the need to be respected by others at all times. At their weakest, if the Threes do not feel they are gaining the respect they deserve they can become very competitive, winning at all cost. In excess, they can become deceptive and vindictive. Image is everything and they will seek to protect their image of success even where the reality is different. To be seen to have failed would be their worst nightmare, and they will seek to preserve their image of success.

Chapter 11: How Others Perceive You

This chapter has been designed to help you understand how others perceive you. As you read this chapter, you will be able to understand why people react to you in a particular manner. You will also understand why you always get the same response from people when you seek clarification.

Structure

The Enneagram's structure might look sophisticated, though it is quite straightforward. It will assist you in how to perceive the Enneagram of the personality of other people if you try to draw it yourself. You must also create a mental picture of the Enneagram of Personalities. When you do that, you will be able to associate people with certain behaviors, and you will also be able to match people who can have a relationship together without having any mind-reading ability or superpower or psyche knowledge.

Draw a circle and mark 9 equal points on its circumference. Designate every purpose by variety from one to 9, with 9 at the highest, for symmetry and by convention. Each purpose represents one among the 9 fundamental temperament sorts.

The 9 points on the circumference are connected with one another by the inner lines of the Enneagram. Note that points 3 and 6, associate with nine point on a regular polygon. The remaining six point area unit connected within the following order: One connects with Four, Four with 2, Two with Eight, Eight with Five, Five with Seven, and Seven with One. These six points form an irregular hexagram. The names of those inner lines are going to be mentioned shortly. As you read along, you will get to understand it better.

The Enneagram: Your Basic Personality Type

From one particular point of reading, the Enneagram is seen as a group of 9 distinct temperament sorts, with each number on the Enneagram denoting one type. It is common to search out a bit of yourself, altogether 9 of the categories, though one among them ought to stand out as being nearest to yourself. This is your basic personality type.

Everyone emerges from childhood with one among the 9 sorts dominating their temperament, with inborn temperament and alternative pre-natal factors being the most determinants of our kind. This is one space wherever most if not all of the key Enneagram authors agreed. Subsequently, this inborn orientation, for the most part, determines the ways that within which we, human beings, have a tendency to learn to adapt to our babyhood atmosphere. It also appears to steer, and sometimes stir, unconscious orientations toward our parental figures. However, why this is often so, we do not. Therefore, we have a tendency to not grasp what governs our behavior. In any case, by the time kids are four or five years old, their consciousness has developed sufficiently to possess a separate sense of self.

Although, their identity continues to be terribly fluid and oscillating between right and wrong yet they continue to know about the world around them. At this age, kids begin to ascertain themselves and notice ways of fitting into the social community and the world around them on their own.

Thus, the orientation of our temperament reflects the totality of all childhood factors (including genetics) that influenced its development. (For a lot of regarding the organic process patterns of every temperament kind, see the connected section within the kind descriptions in temperament sorts and within the knowledge of the Enneagram. Let us look at some points that are germane to enneagram.

The following points are very essential to know the differences between enneagram groups:

People do not really change from one primary personality type to another overnight.

The descriptions of the enneagram of personality types are universal and apply equally to both genders since no type is inherently good or bad or feminine or masculine in nature.

Not all things in the description of your primary type will apply to you every time because you continuously oscillate between the healthy, average, and unhealthy traits that form your personality and types.

The Enneagram makes use of different numbers to designate each of the types because numbers are actually value-neutral. The numbers express the whole range of different attitudes & behaviors of each type without stating anything, whether positive or negative about the type being talked about. Unlike the tags used in psychedelic medicine, numbers provide neutral, shorthand way of indicating a lot about a person without any prejudice whatsoever.

The ranking of the number of particular types is not significant. A larger range is not any higher than a smaller range; it's not higher to be a 9 than a 2 as a result of 9 may be a more significant number in some cases.

No type is naturally better or worse than any other types, so you can say one is better than the other. While all the temperament sorts have distinctive assets and liabilities, some sorts area unit typically thought of to be a lot more fascinating than others in any given culture or cluster.

In addition to the above, for some specific reasons, you may not be happy being a particular type because of the negativities attached to it. You may feel that your kind is "restricted" in some ways. As you learn many things about all the categories, you will understand that just as each has unique capacities in one way or the other, each has different limitations. If you look at areas, content, units, teachings, courses, and discussions on enneagram in a lot of prestigious Western society and their school, you will see some higher development than in other schools and society. This is because of the qualities that society decides to reward, not because of any superior value of those types that we have been discussing so far. The main idea and goal is for you to upgrade and become your best self and become a better version of yourself and not to copy the strengths of any other group of personality.

Identifying Your Basic Personality Type

Although there are some other software and social code personality software available in the market. There are many ways through which you can understand your personality without using any software because they might not be accurate in most cases.This section is designed, so you will have a primary understanding of the categories in this book while not having to use any software or travel to see any psyche, mind reader or read longer descriptions about enneagram of personality.

As you think that regarding your temperament, that which type of the following nine roles fits you best most of the time and describe your personality, I am happy to tell you that you will be able to know where you belong in a short time.

Or, to put it succinctly, if you were to describe your personality or self in a few sentences, which of the following word clusters would come closest to describing the person you think you are?

The Enneagram diagnosis questions

These one-word descriptors are grouped into four-word sets of traits and personalities. Keep in mind, and do not forget that these words highlight and don't represent the total spectrum of every kind of enneagram, and the words are just to give a glimpse of who you are.

Type One is principled, purposeful, self-controlled, and perfectionistic.

Type Two is generous, people-pleasing, demonstrative, and possessive.

Type Three is adaptable, excelling, driven, and image-conscious.

Type Four is expressive, self-absorbed, dramatic, and temperamental.

Type Five is perceptive, innovative, secretive, and isolated.

Type Six is engaging, anxious, responsible, and suspicious.

Type Seven is spontaneous, versatile, acquisitive, and scattered.

Type Eight is self-confident, decisive, willful, and confrontational.

Type Nine is receptive, reassuring, complacent, and resigned.

Chapter 12: The Enneagram Personality

Type 6 - The Loyalist

This personality type is also called the Buddy or The Devil's Advocate. This personality type is very insecure because he or she is often conflicted between trust and distrust and feels very unsteady because of this internal war. Therefore, this person is often very fearful or anxious. As a result, this personality type longs to feel secure and supported.

What Makes the Loyalist a Great Personality

THE LOYALIST IS A PROBLEM SOLVER. This person worries a lot and thinks that everything that can go wrong, will go wrong. As a result, type 6s rarely have peace of mind and are not prone to bouts of spontaneity. This person is very good at troubleshooting because they are often able to see a problem from different points of view. The Loyalist's mind is one that can be a wonderful asset professionally or personally when it is used appropriately. Because this type of personality is so well-equipped at anticipating problems and finding solutions, they are often prepared for any contingency. They are great at developing structures, systems, and ideas for the things that can go wrong and are often the glue that holds organizations together. Type 6s make great and effective leaders when they can channel the multi-faceted way that their mind works in the right way.

THE LOYALIST IS LOYAL. When type 6s enter a relationship, they do not trust easily until that person has proven his or herself. Once they have been given that proof however, they are steadfast in their loyalty. While this can certainly be a good foundation for a relationship, it can do the Loyalists more harm than good sometimes because they stay in a friendship, job, or romantic relationship even when there are signs that they should move on.

THE LOYALIST IS A COMMUNITY BUILDER. Because they are responsible, trustworthy, self-sacrificing, and reliable, this personality type can create security and stability in the communities around them. They are also very dedicated to the movements they believe in.

The Deadly Sins of the Loyalist

THE LOYALIST IS ANXIOUS. The root of the problems that type 6 experiences stems from the fact that they have lost touch with their own inner guidance and authority and seek to project that control and authority onto someone else. They do not trust themselves and fundamentally lack faith in their abilities to make the right decisions. Because of the sense of impending doom that they have, they often test their relationships both professionally and personally and create a self-fulfilling prophecy of failure.

THE LOYALIST IS INSECURE. Because this person is often torn between trust and mistrust, they are often seeking someone or something that they can believe in that is usually not their own selves. Because they lack that inner guidance, they shuffle back and forth between influence until an influence gains their trust.

THE LOYALIST HAS LOW SELF-CONFIDENCE. Because the Loyalist has this deep-seated need to believe in someone or something, this may give rise to issues of authority as they are often looking to turn over that authority to an external source. They do this because they do not believe that they have the internal knowhow to handle life's challenges by themselves. Also, because they are thinking types, they have issues connecting with their inner guidance system. Therefore, they doubt their own minds and judgment easily.

How Loyalists Relate to Other Personality Types

Loyalists vs. Type 1s

Please see Chapter 2: How Reformers Relate to Other Personality Types: Reformers vs. Type 6s.

Loyalists vs. Type 2s

Please see Chapter 3: How Helpers Relate to Other Personality Types: Helpers vs. Type 6s.

Loyalists vs. Type 3s

Please see Chapter 4: How Performers Relate to Other Personality Types: Performers vs. Type 6s.

Loyalists vs. Types 4s

Please see Chapter 5: How Artists Relate to Other Personality Types: Artists vs. Type 6s.

Loyalists vs. Types 5s

Please see Chapter 6: How Observers Relate to Other Personality Types: Observers vs. Type 6s.

Loyalists vs. Type 7s

These are both mental types and can enjoy mentally stimulating each other with natering, humor, and verbal sparring. They make an effective team because type 6s are great at implementation while type 7s are great at generating new ideas. These two personality types help reinforce each other's strengths in a healthy relationship. Problems may arise when type 7s, who are frightful and do not like to be tied down do not give the type 6s the commitment they crave.

Loyalists vs. Type 8s

These two personality types have issues with trust so when they are able to develop a relationship with a strong foundation, they remain solid. Since they are both mental types, they also bring analytical thinking, foresight, and problem-solving skills to the table. Problems may develop because both these personality types are also emotional but tend to hide their emotions. This can of course foster issues in any type of relationship.

Loyalists vs. Type 9s

Type 6s are often confused with type 9s; however, the difference lies in that type 9s are able to trust in others more easily. Nonetheless, the relationship between the two types is very common and stable because both crave stability and predictability. They can build a relationship on dependable value and hard, honest work. The conflict can come into play because both of these personality types find it hard to emotionally express themselves and can easily become withdrawn.

How a Loyalist Can Improve His or Her Life

The biggest part of improving your life as a Loyalist is to deeply introspect so that you can find your own inner guidance. You need to learn to be more in tune with your inner voice and to trust in that internal guidance. A Loyalist needs to practice making decisions even if they do not have all the answers and move forward without second-guessing themselves.

In addition to practicing root and navel chakra, The Loyalist can practice third eye chakra meditation to gain more power into your own insight. This can also help you establish your own belief systems so that you can rely more on your own judgment. The practice of this kind of chakra meditation involves putting your hand in front of the body just below the breasts so that the middle fingers are straight and touch at the tips, pointing forward. Bend the other fingers so that they touch at the upper two phalanges. The thumbs need to point toward the chest and touch at the tips. Chant while concentrating on the third eye chakra, which is at the point slightly between the eyebrows.

When it comes to acupressure, in addition to stimulating the points SP-6 and KI-6, the points KI-3 and KI-4 can also be stimulated. KI-3 is located on the inside of the foot halfway between the ankle bone and the Achilles tendon. The stimulation of this point helps heal the body from the effects of fear. KI-4 is located on the inside of the foot closer to the Achilles tendon than the ankle bone. Stimulating this point helps this personality type feel more sure of themselves.

In addition, the Loyalist can improve his or her life by:

●Developing the understanding that everyone experiences anxiety and accepting that it is a normal part of life. The exploration will allow for the development of ways to manage it.

●Exploring healthy ways for stress management such as exercise and better quality sleep instead of relying on unhealthy dependencies like alcohol and drugs.

●Practicing deep breathing exercises to dispel anxiety.

●Becoming more aware of your tendency to become pessimistic and to steer away from dark moods.

●Learning to identify what makes you most anxious to prevent from overreacting.

●Realizing that most situations are not as bad as they seem and managing your thoughts so that they do not desolate you.

●Working on being more trusting by taking more risks and confronting your fears in relationship development.

●Telling people how you truly feel about them.

Chapter 13: The Sixth Personality

The sixth personality type of the Enneagram is the Loyalist. Also known as the Skeptic or Loyal, the sixth personality is given its name because they are loyal to those close to them as well as their beliefs. Compared to the other types, loyalists tend to have longer-lasting relationships, sticking with people through thick and thin. They have an abundance of commitment and are all about security. Because of their tendency to keep their relationships, they are very reliable and trustworthy.

The description of Loyalists

People of the sixth personality are completely devoted. People, ideas, systems, doctrine; whatever they choose to be bonded to, they bond to, regardless of what might be against the adherence. Sometimes their beliefs do not necessarily align with those already laid down and hence might seem a little rebellious;

however, this won't stop them from pushing limits for those beliefs.

Loyalists fight more for their beliefs than for themselves. They would also fight for anyone they feel stands up for those beliefs. This quality makes them amazing friends, and as long as the other party keeps showing support, they too will remain loyal to the end.

The primary reason for their unwavering loyalty to others is that they fear abandonment. They have little confidence in their own singular abilities and would prefer to have continuous support. This lack of faith doesn't necessarily mean that they never think about making decisions. Quite the contrary, they do - and they do it a lot. They do a lot of worrying about making decisions; hence, the need to be supported.

Despite the search for support, they try to avoid letting others make important decisions and forcing it on them. They like to feel supported/assisted and not controlled. While they are afraid of others forcing decisions on them, they still wouldn't want anything that puts them at the battlefront. They have second thoughts about some things, if not all things and find it hard to decide, especially when those decisions will have an effect on a lot more things and people than them.

They are always trying to build walls against their insecurity. They have so many things that make them feel anxious, and so they look for ways to lock those anxieties out, including finding solace in the many friends that they're loyal to. When they feel the walls will hold, and their friends will stand for them, their level of confidence will increase, and they will be more willing to take part more in decision-making activities.

As soon as they feel their level of support depleting in any way, their self-doubt and anxieties creep back in. When on their own, they are always in a struggle to find a way to stand on their own but finding that stance can turn them into some of the most courageous people.

People of the sixth personality tend to get attached. Their attachment is not only to people but also to ideologies and doctrines that they think to give them most strength. They require a feeling of solidity in their lives. Continually fearing that situations change makes them stick with the beliefs as something to always guide and support them when at a loss of human guidance. When they achieve a sense of stability -which they tend to find hard to do- they do not question it and would prefer that others do not as well. Once they achieve trust in others, they would move heaven and earth to make sure that the connection is maintained with the person. Such people might be in the position of a role model, teacher or close friend — anyone they can see as a paragon in whatever field.

Although it's been said that they are hesitant, people of the sixth personality can also be strong, aggressive, and defendant about what they believe in. A need to prove their loyalty can make them very courageous and forward. They are committed, reliable and due to their constant criticism of everything, they foresee problems and hence help prevent or solve them.

There are many well-known people of this personality including Mark Twain, Robert F. Kennedy, Malcolm X, George H. W. Bush, Prince Harry, Mike Tyson, Eminem, Marilyn Monroe, Woody Allen, Julia Roberts, Jennifer Aniston, Ben Affleck, and Ellen Degeneres.

Challenges of the sixth personality of the Enneagram

Lack of self confidence

People of the sixth personality have very little faith in their prowess or ability. They also belittle their own judgment, conclusions, and convictions. This is why they rely so much on others and beliefs and need external support. They fear that being made to do or decide things will lead to total disaster. However, when these people have any form of stance, they continuously work on making their abilities known. They try to ensure that they receive credit for their hard work.

Being alone

Without any help or guidance, people of the sixth personality mostly float around indecisively and will find it hard to get anything at all done. If they do get things done, they spend a lot of time criticizing and belittling what they have done. Loyalists refuse to believe anything they do on their own would be enough and instead live by the phrase 'strength in numbers.' But when they feel supported or, are convinced of their abilities after a lot of critiquing, their fight changes from that of a need for support to a need to prove themselves.

Need to avoid confrontations

They do not like when they are told they aren't good enough or haven't done enough or that their ideas are worthless. They already do enough by doubting themselves and do not need anymore.

Loyalists fear people finding faults in what they do or their thoughts, so they like to know they have back up and do constant self-evaluation making sure they find errors and solutions in those faults before anyone else does.

Overthinking

When they do things on their own, they always fear that they won't do well. Overthinking and constant critiquing and re-evaluation of themselves, their activities and thoughts is the only way they believe they can find faults before anyone else does. Their brains work overtime in hopes that they will encounter problems before anyone else might notice. When making decisions, they have a lot of second thoughts and would prefer to know that there's some form of back up. The overtime working their brains to make them excellent troubleshooters but deprives them of peace and a feeling of security.

Overachieving

They tend to want to do more than they can. This is mostly because they think the world expects a lot more from them than they can give. Rather than stick to what they can do with ease, they would rather believe that all they've done is way too little. They give their all while thinking there's more to be done.

Attachment

When they find people or ideologies that they believe make them stand firm and provide enough support, they risk getting attached. They would go to great lengths to ensure they keep these connections and beliefs and uphold them no matter what they might be risking. Sometimes, they eventually find it hard if they have to do anything without support from these people or beliefs which make them unable to achieve things on their own. They become very dependent and guarded when approached about it.

Insecurity

The feeling that there is nothing that'll remain sturdy for them to hold on to is a battle that Loyalists face all the time. Their vulnerability manifests in various forms such as anxiety, withdrawal, antisocial behavior, and avoiding leadership roles. Trust is hard for them, and they would rather be on their own, avoiding friendships and spontaneous activities. Loyalists would never delve into anything if they haven't thought and had second thoughts about it first.

It's not like they are boring, but the fear that something might go wrong at any time with anything rules them and makes them retreat from situations and things they have little or no knowledge about. When they are convinced and develop a sense of security, they begin to come out and take more chances if they feel supported. When a person proves supportive of them, they feel safe and develop this sense of courage that would make them go the extra mile for that person.

There you have it. In case you find yourself in this particular type of personality trait, then you now know the challenges you might likely face with time. Therefore, allowing you to find and create surprising ways to cross over these obstacles and become a better version of yourself. Be that as it may, being a loyalist is not such a bad idea after all.

Chapter 14: Type Three – The Achiever

Enneagram Type 3 - The Performer

Threes are feeling-based sorts; however, they channel their passionate vitality into completing things. They step up to the plate and make a solid effort to achieve their objectives. They are profoundly versatile, and they exceed expectations at "getting a handle on" and meeting the desires for others when that will lead them to progress. They like to remain dynamic and, in a hurry so it's difficult to stop or back off. Their emphasis on keeping up their picture and accomplishing results can impede individual needs and wellbeing.

American business is an especially solid Three culture where entertainers get a ton of encouraging feedback for being gainful and productive. A peril for Threes is focusing on outer acclaim or material prizes while losing contact with who they are inside. It's hard for them to step out of their jobs, feel their very own emotions, and choose for themselves what is significant.

Qualities: Successful, fiery, high achiever

Issues: Over worked, eager, focused

Talking style: Enthusiastic, spurring themselves as well as other people for progress

Lower enthusiastic propensity: Vanity, in view of keeping up a decent picture and continually being fruitful

Higher feeling: Truthfulness, which is the eagerness to go past appearances and create individual credibility

Model test: To relinquish picture and social persona and locate one's internal quintessence

Mental resistances: Threes utilize the guard system of recognizable proof to evade disappointment and keep up a mental self-view of being "effective." (Identification is a sort of inescapable pretending and losing oneself in picture).

Substantial examples: As feeling types who put everything into efficiency and results, Threes can collect a great deal of strain around their chest and heart. They are the first "Type A's" and need to look out for early coronary failures or a debilitated invulnerable framework. Underneath a solid layer of chest strain there is generally profound trouble from loss of contact with the internal identity.

Type Three in a word

Threes are confident, alluring, and enchanting. Aggressive, capable, and vivacious, they can likewise be status-cognizant and profoundly determined for progression. They are conciliatory and balanced, yet can likewise be excessively worried about their picture and what others consider them. They normally have issues with workaholism and intensity. At their Best: self-tolerating, credible, all that they appear to be—good examples who motivate others.

Fundamental Fear: Of being useless

Fundamental Desire: To feel important and beneficial

Enneagram Three with a Two-Wing: "The Charmer"

Enneagram Three with a Four-Wing: "The Professional"

Key Motivations: Want to be avowed, to separate themselves from others, to have consideration, to be appreciated, and to dazzle others.

The Meaning of the Arrows (in short)

While moving in their Direction of Disintegration (stress), driven Threes abruptly become separated and unconcerned at Nine. In any case, while moving in their Direction of Integration (development), vain, beguiling Threes become progressively helpful and focused on others, as sound Sixes. Get familiar with the bolts.

Models: Augustus Caesar, Emperor Constantine, Bill Clinton, Tony Blair, Prince William, Condoleeza Rice, Arnold Schwarzenegger, Carl Lewis, Muhammed

Ali, John Edwards, Mitt Romney, Bill Wilson (AA Founder), Andy Warhol, Truman Capote, Werner Erhard, Oprah Winfrey, Deepak Chopra, Tony Robbins, Bernie Madoff, Bryant Gumbel, Michael Jordan, O.J. Simpson, Tiger Woods, Lance Armstrong, Elvis Presley, Paul McCartney, Madonna, Sting, Whitney Houston, Jon Bon Jovi, Lady Gaga, Taylor Swift, Justin Bieber, Brooke Shields, Cindy Crawford, Tom Cruise, Barbra Streisand, Ben Kingsley, Jamie Foxx, Richard Gere, Ken Watanabe, Will Smith, Courteney Cox, Demi Moore, Kevin Spacey, Reese Witherspoon, Anne Hathaway, Chef Daniel Boulud, Dick Clark, Ryan Seacrest, Cat Deeley, Mad Men's "Wear Draper," Glee's "Rachel Berry"

Type Three Overview

We have named character type Three The Achiever since when they are sound, Threes truly can and do accomplish incredible things on the planet. They are the "stars" of human instinct, and individuals regularly admire them on account of their benevolence and individual achievements. Solid Threes great skill is that they want to create themselves and contribute their capacities to the world, and furthermore appreciate inspiring others to more prominent individual accomplishments than others suspected they were prepared to do. They are typically very much respected and famous among their companions, the sort of individual who is every now and again casted a ballot "class president" or "home coming sovereign" since individuals feel they need to be related with this sort of individual who goes about as a sub for them. Sound Threes epitomize the best in a culture, and others can see their deepest desires reflected in them.

Threes are frequently fruitful and popular in light of the fact that, of the considerable number of types, they most have confidence in themselves and in building up their abilities and limits. Threes go about as living "good examples" and paragons on account of their exceptional exemplification of socially esteemed characteristics. Sound Threes realize that they merit the exertion it takes to be "as well as can be expected be." Their prosperity at doing so motivates others to put resources into their very own self-improvement.

Threes need to ensure their lives are a triumph, anyway that is characterized by their family, their way of life, and their social circle. In certain families, achievement implies having a ton of cash, an excellent house, another, costly vehicle, and different materialistic trifles. Others esteem thoughts, and accomplishment to them implies separating oneself in scholarly or logical universes. Achievement in different circles may mean getting renowned as an entertainer, or model, or author, or as an open figure or some likeness thereof, maybe as a government official. A strict family may urge a youngster to turn into a clergyman, minister, or rabbi since these callings have status in their locale and according to the family. Regardless of how achievement is characterized, Threes will attempt to become someone critical in their family and their locale. They won't be "no one important."

To this end, Threes figure out how to perform in manners that will earn them recognition and positive consideration. As youngsters, they figured out how to perceive the exercises that were esteemed by their folks or companions, and put their energies into exceeding expectations in those exercises. Threes additionally figured out how to develop and build up whatever about them is appealing or conceivably great.

Everybody needs consideration, support, and the confirmation of their incentive so as to flourish, and Threes are the sort which most epitomizes this widespread human need. Threes need achievement less for the things that achievement will purchase (like Sevens), or for the power and sentiment of autonomy that it will bring (like Eights). They need achievement since they fear vanishing into a gap of void and uselessness: without the expanded consideration and sentiment of achievement which achievement generally brings, Threes dread that they are no one and have no worth.

The issue is that, in the fast hurry to accomplish whatever they accept will make them progressively significant, Threes can turn out to be so estranged from themselves that they never again recognize what they genuinely need, or what their genuine emotions or interests are. In this state, they are simple prey to self–misdirection, misleading, and wrongness of different types. Along these lines, the more profound issue is that their quest for an approach to be of significant worth progressively removes them further from their very own Essential Self with its center of genuine worth. From their most punctual years, as Threes become subject to accepting consideration from others and in seeking after the qualities that others reward, they step by step put some distance between themselves. Bit by bit, their own internal center, their "profound longing," is deserted until they never again remember it.

Consequently, while they are the essential kind in the Feeling Center, Threes, strikingly, are not known as "feeling" individuals; rather, they are individuals of activity and accomplishment. Maybe they "put their emotions in a container" so they can excel with what they need to accomplish. Threes have come to accept that feelings impede their exhibition, so they substitute reasoning and pragmatic activity for sentiments.

Threes report that when they understand to what degree they have adjusted their lives to the desires for other people, the inquiry emerges, "Well, at that point, what do I need?" They regularly just didn't have any acquaintance with; it was anything but an inquiry that had ever come up previously. In this manner, the crucial predicament of Threes is that they have not been permitted to be who they truly are and to show their very own real characteristics. At a youthful age, they got the message that they were not permitted to have emotions and act naturally: they should, as a result, be another person to be acknowledged. Somewhat, the entirety of the character types have been sent a similar message, but since of their specific foundation and cosmetics, Threes not just heard it, they started to live by it. The consideration they got by performing with a specific goal in mind was their oxygen, and they required it to relax. Lamentably, it came at a significant expense.

Type Three—Levels of Development

Solid Levels

Level 1 (At Their Best): Self-tolerating, inward coordinated, and valid, all that they appear to be. Humble and beneficent, self-deprecatory humour and a totality of heart develop. Delicate and generous.

Level 2: Self-guaranteed, vivacious, and able with high confidence: they put stock in themselves and their very own worth. Versatile, alluring, enchanting, and generous.

Level 3: Ambitious to develop themselves, to be "as well as can be expected to be"— frequently gotten exceptional, a human perfect, exemplifying broadly respected social characteristics. Exceptionally successful: others are roused to resemble them in some positive manner.

Normal Levels

Level 4: Highly worried about their exhibition, carrying out their responsibility well, always driving self to accomplish objectives as though self-esteem relies upon it. Startled of disappointment. Contrast self as well as other people in look for status and achievement. Become careerists, social climbers, put resources into eliteness and being the "best."

Level 5: Become picture cognizant, exceptionally worried about how they are seen.

Chapter 15: Spiritual Consciousness

Can your personality type alter the way you understand spiritual consciousness?

The concept of spiritual consciousness was established in German Idealism and is

a central belief in modern, common spirituality. Higher consciousness is

the knowledge of a higher Self, inspirational reality, or God. Most simply, it is the

part of an individual that is capable of rising above natural instincts. As noted, the

Enneagram gives us the understanding and knowledge to analyze our basic

instincts and personality traits. The short answer is, yes!

Mysticism or spirituality is not restricted to a single religion. It matures in us

within the context of the religious customs, principles, and era which have shaped our lives. The journey to spiritual consciousness is filled with moments in darkness

without seeing the light until long after the darkness is overcome.

The journey begins when an individual experiences an awakening from their

personal ego into a higher, transcendent perspective. This moment also brings

awareness to one's self and misery. Ultimately, while we suffer, we are stripped of

everything but faith. Our faith becomes our only guide and connects us to mystery.

It is then that we surrender.

When life hands us a bad turn, it is sometimes hard to believe in faith, mysticism

and blessings. It is hard to find the positive in a bad situation but it is always there.

The Enneagram can help you learn more about yourself and how you handle

disappointment or tragedy. These times in our life give us the opportunity to rise above, have faith and keep going. Sometimes, those are the only chances we have

to become a better person.

The nine Enneagram types have a varied perspective on the world. One can

characterize their view as:

☐ Perfectionist: I feel loved/safe when I am good.

☐ Assistant: I feel loved/safe when I am generous.

☐ Doer: I feel loved/safe when I am effective.

☐ Eccentric: I feel loved/safe when I am exceptional.

☐ Observer: I feel loved/safe when I am independent.

☐ Loyal Skeptic: I feel loved/safe when I am authentic.

☐ Epicure: I feel loved/safe when I am cheerful.

☐ Boss: I feel loved/safe when I am influential.

☐ Mediator: I feel loved/safe when I am helpful.

During this time, we are forced to embrace a purification from our own instinctual behaviors. Each type will have a different challenge to overcome in this process.

☐ Perfectionist: To discover excellence, crave its control in nothing.

☐ Assistant: To discover acceptance, crave its control in nothing.

☐ Doer: To discover achievement, crave its control in nothing.

☐ Eccentric: To discover connection, crave its possession in nothing.

☐ Observer: To acquire knowledge you do not have, embrace the unknown.

☐ Loyal Skeptic: To discover safety, crave its possession in nothing.

☐ Epicure: To discover all that is imaginable, embrace limiting the possible.

☐ Boss: To discover authority, embrace weakness.

☐ Mediator: To discover unification, embrace diversity in all things.

Our view has now shifted and we have revealed a new virtue. We survive and realize

that there is a divine process. The reality is that not everyone comes out of a trial

unscathed. Some may lose their sense of religion, faith in God or in mysticism. It

is therefore quite possible for someone to lose themselves in tragedy. Some are

engrossed in the events their living through that there is no room for reflection.

For those that come closer to their spiritual consciousness they feel loved and in

turn, put love back in to the world. Our experiences are the heart of the spiritual

world. However, our knowledge of religion comes from those in higher social

classes. Much of the history of Christianity is told from a man's perspective and their understanding of a woman's role and experience.

More modern research focuses on the ordinary individual, not just the elite.

Additionally, there are findings that show a correlation between Enneagram type

and their changes through Spiritual Consciousness.

The Perfectionist's vice is anger while its virtue is serenity. The stress that comes

from believing they must correct themselves and everyone else is denied and they

find compassion. Their idea of mysticism is perfect Holiness and that it is a

continuous process and may not mirror the human structure of it.

The Assistant's vice is pride and its virtue is humility. Their exaggerated logic of

pride that comes with helping others to obtain approval gives way to give just

enough while weighing one's own desires and boundaries. Their divine idea is Holy

Will that God's grace is given abundantly and we must meet that same level of

giving in service.

The Doer's vice is deceit and their virtue is honesty. Their false perception that

their image is who they are, instead becomes a more authentic acceptance of limits,

emotions and disappointments. Their divine idea revolves around hope and the

realization that success has a spiritual origin and we must rely on mysticism (God),

not ourselves, to find an optimistic conclusion.

The Eccentric's vice is envy and their virtue is equanimity. Their obsession with

what is absent in ordinary life changes to an awareness that nothing is lacking and

happiness can be found in what we have now. Their divine idea is spiritual origin

in realizing that we are unique and created by God and therefore always connected to a constant source of love.

The Observer's vice is avarice and their virtue is non-attachment. They exhibit a

predisposition to hoarding time, room, views and emotions release and is then an

attitude of sincerity to receive and share life. Their divine idea is knowledge and

appreciating that higher knowing is not achieved by the mind alone, but includes

the body and emotional state.

The Loyal Skeptic's vice is fear and doubt while its virtue is courage. Their fixation

with doubt and curiosity that stimulates the mind to be excessively distrustful and

the imagination to be overactive diminishes and gifts the capacity to perform with

self-confidence that one has power within themselves to developed guidance. Their

divine idea is Faith and knowing they can relax and believe in a divine plan and

their place in it.

The Epicure's vice is gluttony and their virtue is sobriety. They stay preoccupied

with enjoying life by always having a multitude of strategies and progress to one

with focus and devotion with both positivity and negativity equally weighing in on

life. Their divine idea is Holy work and realizing they have a part in a divine plan

and once committed, they must also be willing to accept the restrictions and

defeats of life.

The Boss's vice is lust with a virtue of innocence. Their passion of controlling

everything around them that then causes dominance gives way to a mindfulness of

their own weakness and ability to use power more adequately. Their divine idea is

Holy truth and understanding that mystic truth is much bigger than anything imaginable.

The Mediator's vice is being a sloth while their virtue is right action. They have a

predisposition to lose themselves and their God-given purpose evolves into the

capacity to perform on their own and be more aware of their separate identity and

value. Their divine idea is love and learning that in order to connect with God or

anyone else in a complete love they must have the capacity to identify themselves.

It is largely understood that we reach a level of spiritual consciousness during mid-

life (ages 35-50) after we have experienced many joys and sorrows of life. We

naturally become more aware that we are not alone and that there is a mysticism

that supports us in love. It is in our dark times that we are disconnected from our

own self-image and we evolve either positively or negatively. This change is directly related to our Enneagram type.

Being more aware of ourselves and our personality type can help us to build our

life in a positive way. We are more aware of what are strengths and weaknesses are

so we have the ability to make changes that we want. You have probably heard,

"Knowledge is Power." In the case of the Enneagram, this is especially true. Having

knowledge of our traits, both positive and negative, gives us a unique power.

Chapter 16: The Loyalist

Synopsis

They will remain by you till death. Such is the perfect of a supporter – in the event that you gain their trust, that is...

This section discusses:

• What a follower is about

• Why are followers great to have around

• What is most troublesome about followers

• Dealing with them and drawing out the best

• Who they coexist with

• Who they don't alongside

Championing the reason for unwaveringness, despite even the most forboding circumstances... they WILL remain!

– figure out how to adore them, acknowledge them for who they are and bring the best out of them!

What Is A Loyalist?

A follower is an individual who is exemplified by the celebrated tune "Remain by me". The day they construct strong trust with somebody, they will stick by all of them the path until the end.

They are an exceptionally special kind of individuals in the matter of trust in light of the fact that they have a tendency to trust individuals as much as they doubt individuals in the meantime. These individuals are dependably always searching for something or somebody to put stock in profoundly – once the individuals they have faith in have 'earned their trust', they will be faithful till death.

The Good

The fortunate thing about followers is that they are truly gallant towards individuals who've earned their trust – regularly allegorically tossing themselves before activity to spare them.

Where it counts inside, they need to feel safe – they need to accept that in an unwavering, trusting relationship, there is no apprehension of selling out and will frequently extend these to their trusted individuals, particularly their life accomplices.

They make great life accomplices in the meantime as well.

Having a sacred thought of confidence, they always accept that marvels will happen and despite the fact that the individuals they trust do botch, they will tend to have faith in them until they improve as an individual.

The Bad

Supporters are infrequently fainting girls – feeling frail with individuals around them.

They are so at odds with trust and doubt that it will show up truly clashing now and again (until the individual gains their trust).

They are likewise phobic creatures – anxious about a considerable measure of things. While they may be great at settling issues, they are additionally loaded with tension to the center as they don't generally have true serenity.

Step by step instructions to Deal With Them

Since followers are for the most part apprehensive about disconnection and helplessness, the most ideal route is to constantly quiet them down and solace them – demonstrating to them that you also can be dependable in light of the fact that where it counts inside, they are constantly suspicious of others (thus their obsession with parts and bunches of dependability).

A sparing toward oneself follower will dependably be working alone, discreetly helping other people frightful of individuals finding their need in their being.

The most ideal approach to manage them is to give back their trust and issue them confidence.

A sexual supporter will dependably stick to the mate, however infrequently, being faithful for the wrong things is constantly terrible so concentrate on developing them.

To wrap things up, a social follower is an individual who will dependably stay with a gathering or a cause the distance till the end. They work extremely well with peacemakers (sort 9) who are regularly fortifies their supporter and safe looking for nature and they abhor being around achievers (sort 3) who issues them an inclination of shakiness as it shakes their safe place of security in the meantime.

Chapter 17: Type Six Personality

TYPE SIX (loyalist and skeptic) - As a loyalist, a Type Six long to feel safe and would remain loyal to anyone who can offer them safety in return. As a skeptic, they often have their doubts about everything and need to be sufficiently convinced before putting their trust in a person or thing.

The characteristics of Type Six personality individuals are as follows -

● Individuals with Type Six personality have an inbuilt 'fear- response' to many things around them whether real or imagined. This comes in handy as a protection against dangerous situations as they are quick to spot such situations. Other people around them can deploy them as a sentry because of this natural ability. Such an attribute may also cause them to miss out on vital opportunities in life leading to regrets in the future.

- Being part of the mental or thinking group, Type Six think about almost every step or action they are about to take. And this can sometimes cause them to procrastinate on urgent matters. This may also create an impression that makes people see them as being lazy. A Type Six person often stays clear of self-imposed urgency and prefers to act after contemplating about the next move. They can get things done when they are certain they are on the right path.

- Type Sixes personality individuals are consultative and prefer guidance when they are heading down a path they have not taken in the past. When seeking counsel, they approach those with considerable experience about what they intend to do and it does not matter to them whether the other person is older or as educated as they are. Receiving counsel from others enables them to minimise the risks associated with their proposed plans and decisions.

• Type Six personalities are averse to risk and adventure no matter how rewarding such risks may appear to be. So a typical Six would rather hold on to a job for many years when job and financial guarantees are on the table rather than embark on an entrepreneurial journey that could yield bumper returns. Even when they go into business, they want to get all the facts they can lay their hands on before injecting their hard-earned money.

• Type Sixes are good listeners, they pay rapt attention to those they are conversing with. While listening, they may ask a lot of questions to clarify the discussion. Even when they have got certain information about an issue, they would still want to glean as much as they can from others. This is because gathering adequate and accurate information helps to clear their doubts and make informed decisions.

• Type Sixes personality individuals prefer doing jobs that give them a source of security for the future even when such jobs are not as lucrative as the other available job options. This is why you would find many of the Type Sixes in relatively stable professions like military service and academia. They have no issues with sticking with a single employer for their entire working lives and they may likely slip into depression if they lose their jobs without getting another in a short while.

• These individuals are likely to comply with company rules and policies. Sticking to the instructions of those in authority is not an issue for them as long as they would not be held directly accountable at the end of the day. As long as they can put their faith and trust in their superiors, carrying out their orders become easy. This is the reason why their bosses of Type Sixes often trust them to execute their instructions to the letter with little or no alterations.

• Type Sixes may have difficulty accepting either praise or blame as a result of suspicion. Either way, they may consider both the praise and the blame as tools of manipulation in the hands of the other person. They doubt virtually everything and everyone around them but when they finally overcome such doubts, they hold on tightly to that thing, person or idea.

Below is a list of renowned Type Sixes in human history -

• DAVID LETTERMAN - An American television host, writer, and producer who hosted thousands of late night talk shows for over three decades. He is regarded as one of the greatest television stars of all time and his TV show is also one of the greatest of all time too. As a Type Six, David Letterman is a natural interrogator who had a reputation for being an acerbic interviewer.

• RICHARD NIXON - A former President of the United States, he also served his nation in other positions such as United States Vice President and legislator from California. As a Type Six, Richard Nixon was known to have a very secretive and awkward personality. He liked to distance himself from people especially when he was not sure of what their motives were. His biographer described him as being driven and uneasy with himself in some ways. Richard Nixon felt that he was doomed to be defamed, harassed and under-appreciated but he would ultimately prevail.

- WOODY ALLEN - An American director, writer, comedian and actor whose career spans more than six decades. He has won four Academy Awards and nine British Academy Film Awards. As a comedian, he developed the persona of an insecure and fretful person which he maintains is quite different from his real-life personality. But there are strong indications that this persona is reflective of his true personality.

- TOM CLANCY - An American novelist best known for his literary works that focus on espionage and military science. He has authored 17 bestseller novels with more than copies of them in print. His choice of writing themes was a subtle representation of his Type Six personality. He loved to write about spy networks and military-oriented topics.

- MEL GIBSON - An American actor and filmmaker who is best known for his action hero roles and has received numerous awards both for the roles of an actor and a director. Mel Gibson is a typical Doubting Thomas who is skeptical about most things unless he has adequate facts.

- GEORGE H. W. BUSH - A former President of the United States who also served his country as congressman, ambassador and director of Central Intelligence. He has been actively involved in humanitarian work since he left office. As a Type Six, he was seen as a 'pragmatic caretaker' president who lacked a unified and compelling long-term theme in his efforts. He was constantly wavering between opinions and sometimes found it difficult to take decisive action.

- PAUL NEWMAN - An American actor-director and entrepreneur who has received many awards for his acting performances in movies. He also won several national championships as a race car driver and made a huge impact in the area of philanthropy prior to his demise. His religious inclination gives us a bit of an insight into his Type Six personality; he claimed to be a Jew without identifying with any particular faith or religion.

● TED TURNER - An American media mogul and philanthropist who founded Cable News Network (CNN), the first 24-hour cable news channel. As a philanthropist, he is known for his one billion dollar gift to support the United Nations, which created the United Nations Foundation, a public charity to broaden domestic support for the UN. In university, Ted Turner was not so certain about the course he wanted to study. He initially chose classics before switching to economics. He also finds it relatively difficult to stick with stable religious beliefs. At various points in his life, he has referred to himself as an atheist, agnostic and believer.

The typical roles played by Type Sixes include -

• THE FENCE-SITTER - A regular Type Six would struggle with indecision unless he or she rewires his or her thinking. They are habitual fence-sitters and are slow to commit themselves to a worthy cause due to inner doubts. Things may get worse when they do not relay their doubts to other people for fear of criticism, making it very difficult for others to be of help.

• THE DETECTIVE - Type Sixes can smell a rat where nothing of such exists because of their tendency to suspect everything and everyone. Such un-founded suspicion may accidentally lead to answers that would prove to be useful in the end. Type Sixes must learn to bridle their tongue so as not to offend other people with their questioning and suspicion.

• THE BUDDY - A Type Six can be your close friend and confidant giving you a listening ear when you need someone to talk to. They are likely to maintain your confidence and keep your secrets as a result of their need to secure the relationship from which they derive safety and security.

• THE DOUBTING THOMAS - The number of verifiable facts or information that would convince other people may not be sufficient for a Type Six. They prefer to assess every single bit of detail and get a 110% assurance before getting committed to anything at all.

• THE DEFENDER - As a means of demonstrating their loyalty and reliability, a Type Six is ready to fight in defense of his or her friends, whether they are present or not. They would also expect the same favour in return and this will give them a deep sense of satisfaction in that relationship. This is the kind of relationship that makes them feel safe.

• THE DEVIL'S ADVOCATE - Type Sixes like to play the devil's advocate as a means of provoking the other party in an argument to reveal more information. Sometimes, they could also do this as a way of taking sides (in an argument or heated conversation) with people who are close to them.

● THE LOYALIST - To a certain extent, anyone who is close to a Type Six can count on their unfailing loyalty as long as the other party continues to play their role. When the benefits are cut off, they simply withdraw their loyalty and make it available to someone else. A good example is a Type Six who is loyal to senior political office holders as long as they remain in office but when their fortunes change, a Type Six individual may simply disappear.

● THE INTERROGATOR - It is a well-known fact that children ask a lot of questions, a typical child may ask dozens of questions in a single day. Type Sixes retain this habit even in adulthood and may bore people around them with too many questions. The habit is amplified when they find someone who is willing and able to provide as many answers as possible.

- THE COURAGEOUS HERO - Type Six personality individuals are bold when they have to face dangerous situations. The courage drawn from their initial fears or doubts can inspire them to heroic acts that impresses everyone around.

- THE SECURITY OFFICER - Type Six individuals are usually the first to spot loopholes and vulnerabilities in any setup, whether physical or abstract. They issue repeated warnings even when the perceived threats will not affect them alone or even affect them directly.

Type Sixes are quite difficult to spot via casual observation because of their exceptional ability to pretend and alter their thinking and behavior to suit the situation in which they find themselves. But if you can read between the lines, you would know them by virtue of what they say. Their speech is usually filled with doubts, questions, warnings, and anxieties. Their positive side may reveal a person that is warm, loyal, caring, likable, helpful and responsible. Their negative side may reveal a person that is unpredictable, hyper-vigilant, self-defeating, paranoid and defensive.

The following careers would suit a Type Six personality - most kinds of careers including corporate management, legal practice, quality control, military service, risk management, accounting and academia.

In this chapter, we have examined the following -

● The characteristic features of Type Six personalities

● Famous Type Six personalities in history

● Typical roles that can be played by a Type Six personality

Chapter 18: Type Nine The Peaceful Caregiver

In This Chapter:

Standing up for yourself Developing a separate identity What lies beneath the niceness

Finding your power and your passion

Identifying the Nine in Yourself and Others

Since Nines can imitate any type it can be a challenge to spot a Nine, as they effortlessly alter to adapt to those around them. Their consistent theme is conflict avoidance, with occasional anger eruptions when they repress themselves too much. Never consistently like any other type, Nines are the "nice guys" of the universe.

Nonverbal cues

In keeping with their passive position in life, Nine's movements and gestures are slower than most. More reticent to speak than some other types, they generate connection with others using a good deal of non- verbal communication.

Some of Nine's non-verbal cues include:

When stressed, hands push out like a stop sign

or press down to dampen intensity or loud noises Head nods in agreement

Relaxed settled-in posture when seated

Sometimes distractible with a somewhat spacey facial expression Sometimes a clear-eyed presence with an open gaze

Dressing for comfort

Imitating others' body postures and gestures Overall sense of innocence, sweetness

verbal cues

Nines have interesting verbal habits. They will agree with you but sometimes repeat themselves, usually because they are uncertain you are hearing them. When relaxed and talking about a pleasant topic they can verbally meander. Their words are often low-key, trailing off at the end.

Other verbal cues include:

Slower speech patterns, even-toned or monotone

Expressions such as, "That is so true." "I understand." "I agree." Agreeable conversations

Imitates voice tone of others

Changing the topic to something agreeable

Nines in caregiving

As a Nine, you value peace and harmony above all else, and want everyone to like you and treat you well. Therefore, your identity changes according to the situation at hand and others perceived expectations. Nines identify who they are by identifying with others. If you've caught tantalizing glimpses of yourself in each of the previous types, but none were an exact fit, you may well be a Nine.

To understand the Nine, it is important to know that Nines adapt to the wants of others, accommodate others, and go out of their way to create either real or imagined peace, at least from the Nine perspective. As a Nine, you're generally positive, optimistic, and trusting, although you can get down if you can't create peace. You love life and look for the best in all people and situations.

You might think that accommodating would make caretaking easier, but not necessarily. Any behavioral extreme can undermine caregiving, even niceness. You can be seen as gullible. Others may not trust your perspective or decisions. If you defer too much to others or adapt your ideas too easily to those of others (such as the medical community) you may be too malleable to be effective as an advocate for your Loved One.

Accommodating doesn't necessarily serve you either, as it adds stress to your already stressful journey. You may seem okay on the surface, but always putting other people first allows your resentment to build. When you reach your limit, you slam on the brakes or run for your life. People get confused as to why such an agreeable person is suddenly not so agreeable. The most confused one may be you.

Nine's Positive Traits

Nines are people most people want to know. You are the salt of earth, accepting, forgiving, and generous—the basic good person.

Egalitarian - You have no guile, are generally easy to be with and have a high tolerance for differences in people, making it easier to deal with the many types of professionals and family who come and go throughout caregiving.

Self-sacrificing - You'll easily sacrifice yourself for the unity of the whole, going out of your way to create harmony and connection. Your

flexibility may just end up holding the family together.

Non-Egoic - You are genuinely happy for the successes of others and are willing to learn from them, which can diminish any competition that might arise with siblings.

Grateful - Your appreciation and gratitude for the simple things in life can help others in caregiving to lighten up and focus on the good.

Empathetic - Your ability to see the world through others' eyes and feel what they are feeling gives them great comfort and the experience of being heard.

Even Tempered - Your rarely flare up and can stay on an even keel when others are losing their cool. You are the emotional ballast for others at this time.

Nine's Challenges

Each enneatype protects itself from its own version of stress and the aspects of people and life that each finds uncomfortable. Each defense makes sense, once you understand the type. As a caregiver it is critical to know and manage your habitual coping strategies.

Stress/Avoidance Loop - Nines can find themselves in a self- perpetuating loop of stress and avoidance. If you are a Nine, you only increase your stress by holding it inside instead of releasing it, then distracting yourself with comfort or addictions. But avoiding stress by avoiding risk or repressing your Self creates more internal conflict and avoidance. Eventually your avoidance strategies catch up with you, surfacing as passive-aggressive behaviors.

Making Nice - Nines want so badly for things to go smoothly and for interactions to be pleasant that they completely avoid the realities of the moment. However harsher realities are more prevalent in caregiving and the cost of ignoring the unpleasant carries a bigger price. You simply can't afford to put your head in the sand.

Repressing Anger - Nines typically disown their anger. Instead of saying no or speaking up for yourself, you get stubborn, delay, forget, and can even get more agreeable, yet with no action. When someone asks what's wrong, you respond that everything is fine. Of course everything isn't fine, but you can't break through your veneer of nice to explain.

These patterns are deadly for a family caregiver.

Procrastination - As caregiving demands build, they can reach a point where the typical Nine responds, not with action, but with procrastination. While this may feel relatively good for the moment, in the long run the Nine digs her hole deeper as she becomes indecisive and confused. Needs requiring immediate action can go unaddressed, bringing real danger.

Excessive Self Sacrifice - The experience of invisibility is an earmark of the Nine. At its extreme, a Nine can lose her personal identity, sacrificing everything to her Loved One(s) and family while her self-esteem takes a beating. You can feel lost, at the beck and call of everyone's command or whim, as though life put you under a rock which rarely moves.

Nine's Opportunities for Personal Growth

When fully developed, you are assertive, self-directed, action-oriented, individualistic, passionate, clear, and inspiring in your communication. You are a powerfully effective and balanced caregiver.

Living with Stress - For many Nines the first step in living with stress is just to identify it. To identify it, you need to be looking within yourself rather than outside of yourself (your habitual point of focus.) Self-connection is a challenge for a Nine, so start there, and when you do notice stress building, practice even in little ways venting your feelings or soothing yourself. Sacrifice your familiar survival/avoidance strategies for more useful ones that build your strength.

Telling the Truth - There are key times in caregiving that call for acknowledging the unpleasant or inconvenient, for telling it like it is. Instead of making nice all of the time, practice first telling yourself the truth about people and circumstances. To be ready to respond to the uncomfortable events of caretaking you need to be in touch with what you see as true. Practice acknowledging the less than optimal moments. If your instincts tell you that something is amiss but you're not sure, bounce your doubts off of someone else, perhaps a friend or professional in your area of concern. Your decisiveness may save the day if others have their heads in the sand.

Owning Anger - Telling the truth includes owning and expressing your emotional truth. Anger is normal, and in caregiving, anger can

even be your friend. It is the red flag that can stop your forward motion and external focus to have you asking the important questions. What am I resisting in someone else or in the current circumstances? How can I safely and constructively express my feelings and needs so that I can live with them and move along more easily? What do I need to do for myself to take care of myself? Learn to be direct now to prevent later explosions. (The Caregiver's Compass by Holly Whiteside is a handbook on Amazon with detailed tools for emotional balance).

Personal Effectiveness - Instead of putting off even small caregiving demands, take the pressure off while staying effective. Some new tactics can include doing small tasks right when they come up so that they don't build up. Ask a small group of trusted family or friends to be on call to run interference before you get to overwhelm. Invite a trusted Loved One to partner with you by double checking how you're coping and what tasks are on the front burner.

Being Present - Life, and caregiving at its best, are about growth. Your journey, as a Nine, is to discover who you are as an individual and let go of automatically conforming to others' real or imagined expectations. Verbalize your thoughts and perspective. Maintain your integrity by announcing your place on the care team.

Be more assertive - You let people run roughshod over you and tend to go along to get along way too much. Some people will take as much as they can get, if you don't speak up, define your terms, or say no. Take an assertiveness class and practice speaking up. People will often feel more comfortable with you, when you can define who you are.

Clarify what you want - You tend to stay a bit foggy about what you want and what your goals are. Think about that and state what you want clearly and directly. If you are vague, others will relate vaguely to you. Set goals and don't get distracted by secondary motivations. Don't clean up the tool shed to avoid talking to someone. Talk first, and then organize the tool shed as a reward!

Take action - You tend to think about what you want and then dismiss it. Sometimes you don't clarify, because you are afraid to go into action. Things don't get done, unless you do them. Make the call to find out the information. Find out when the check is supposed to arrive. Make no assumptions. Talk to the person in charge. Don't procrastinate.

Usually, the task you need to do is easier than your imagination thinks it will be.

Make a to-do list right now and do the first task on that list!

Focus on reality - You tend to be in your imagination, hoping, wishing things were different. Pay attention to what is happening and don't go into some wish fulfillment of what might happen. When you express what you want and work toward having it, you find out what is real. You tend to hope something positive will happen, but it won't, if you don't go into gear. Get to first base to get into the game.

Let go of comfort - You love comfort, the known, certain traditions. That is nice, but things change, and there are new challenges. Stay abreast of what is current and live in the now, not the distant or recent past. Let it go, as you tend to hold onto it. Enjoy your comforts—food, your favorite TV show, comfortable clothes, your hot toddy—but be open to new comforts. Adjust and make changes to the changing world. Make a list of the changes you need to respond to.

Find your own backbone. Redefine yourself as tough, in addition to being nice. It is great to be the sweet, kind, nice person you are, but unfortunately it doesn't always work to your advantage. Understand there is aggression in the world and you must respond in some way. Fight for justice and speak out. Be a protester and confront situations that are against your values.

Accept anger and conflict - You tend to avoid conflict at all costs, but conflict is natural and can help in personal development. The more you clearly define yourself, the less conflict you may have with others. People get more upset with you when you are unclear, indirect, and angry under the surface. Accept anger as a natural emotion that helps define how you feel, what you want, and what you won't put up with. Be your true self, not just your pacifying self, and you'll feel more whole. What do you need to face today?

The Nine's Heart, Soul, and Mind

Nines in Relationships

In our culture, caregivers start from the weakened position of invisibility, tending only to their Loved One's needs. This culturalbias

makes caregiving doubly hard for Nines, who tend to feel invisible at the best of times. Conflict avoidance is so much your nature that you can maintain unhealthy or unworkable relationships for a long time. Being knee-jerk positive while overlooking your own needs can be a recipe for a caregiving disaster, yet if you seek change, you risk conflict. Burying your head in the sand of denial can seem to be the only alternative to discomfort. It is a double bind that can have you go on, and on, and on.

Since your tendency is also to avoid setting self-goals that conflict with others, you run the risk of suffocating in caregiving while sacrificing your passion for life. On one hand you love life and want to be the best caregiver, but on the other you retreat from bringing yourself into the picture. Yet curiously, laid back Nines often attract those with opposite qualities, the more direct or anger-oriented types. These model for you the skills that you need. As you accept your own anger and are more direct, you more consciously develop the relationships that will truly serve you during caregiving. Keep seeing yourself as the powerful person that you are and make the choices that suit you, behind which you can stand.

The same qualities—empathy, acceptance, a forgiving nature, tolerance, inclusiveness—that make you so wonderful in certain aspects of care relating, can be your weak spot in others. To up the stakes even higher, Nines often attract people with opposite qualities, the more direct, or anger-oriented types. So, you tend to build your sense of self by going along with or responding to others, instead of being the initiator. You might have gotten away with that before caregiving, but now there are times when you must take a stand.

Relationship Advice - The problem is not so much that you're holding back, it is that you're better at knowing what you don't think or want than what you do. Clarify what you think and want. Be more self-sourced and self-defined so that you will know when action is necessary. You and your Loved One will feel more secure and better balanced.

Go more for what you know you need and take the risks that might actually expand your relationship with your Loved One or a sibling. Don't take the easier but more destructive paths of avoidance when conflict is too overwhelming. Listen carefully to your inner signals and seek some support when extreme fear or surfacing anger calls for it.

When you accept your own anger and are more direct, you can

consciously find or foster the relationships that will serve you during caretaking. Keep seeing yourself as the powerful person that you are and make the choices that suit you, behind which you can stand.

Nine's Spiritual Side

You are not a skeptic. You innately sense the Oneness of all life and want to make the world a better place for everyone. The Golden Rule guides your action—you do go out of your way to help others in need without requiring special recognition for your efforts. You have a clear awareness of how life should be lived. As a Nine, you see life as good and believe human greed and selfishness are aberrations. You may attend church or belong to groups that emphasize the spiritual aspects of life. Many mystics and psychics are Nines.

A Spiritual Lesson - You are so good at helping others that eventually your own spirit can become impoverished. If, indeed, All is One, you are a part of that One. By focusing on the life of your own spirit you balance your spirituality and become more fully ready to honor your place in your spiritual community.

How Nines Think & Make Decisions

Nines, like all the types, have an inner dialogue going on that reflects their type values. Often, with Nines, what you see on their calm surface is not an accurate indicator of the conflict that simmers beneath. Nines struggle with an inner life that scares them to share.

The quintessential question for you is, Who am I, really? As a Nine, you struggle with establishing your unique identity. This is difficult, as your natural tendency is to mold yourself to fit whomever you're with, which can be tiring, and counterproductive work. Seeing all sides of an issue, while lacking a strong core self, makes decision-making difficult. Everything seems fairly equal in value and weight. So, you freeze up and often wait until the last minute to let someone else or even fate decide for you.

It is hard to trust that you can be in control of your life and decide for yourself and not have to take care of or pacify everyone else. It is a full time job keeping peace, particularly when you are the main person needing it.

Typical Nine thoughts include: It is best to compromise.

I need to get those two to stop arguing. Maybe I can fix it. I'll try to give you what you need.

Selfishness makes me so angry!

I can't figure out what I want. It is hard to know what to do.

Nine's Thought/Action Alternatives

As a Nine, communicating what you want is essential for growth. You need to accept your thinking, and have the courage to use that thinking to speak out what you previously dared not say.

Good decision-making comes from understanding that you are an individual, with individual wants and needs. Once you understand that, you can factor in the needs of your Loved One.

True peace is about a decision and commitment to act on your values, even in the face of a very non-peaceful and conflicted situation. To grow, Nines need to face the realities of life and human nature—selfishness, resentment, jealousy—while trying to do only what you can to help your Loved One and others with acceptance, unity, and peace. The Serenity Prayer for acceptance, courage and wisdom would be a good guide. Of course, unless you can make your own decisions based on personal values, it is difficult to help others.

Thoughts that caregiver Nines may find helpful are: That doesn't work for me.

I hope you two can resolve this. I need to go take care of myself. You're asking for more than I can give.

I hear your needs, and I have some too.

I'm going to take my time to figure out what feels right to me.

Making the Most of Being A Nine

Nine's modifiers bring skills that help Nine to get clarity on who they can be in the world.

Nine's Stress Type - Cautious Six

Growth Type - Achieving Three

Nine's Stress Type Six, (The Cautious Caregiver) manifests itself in a tendency to be stuck in fear, obsession, and even paranoia. But Nine is a Body type, and needs to reconnect to the body when in fear, rather than mentally ruminate about worst-case scenarios like the Head type Six. If you are a Nine, focus on action and bring the fear along, if necessary. Trust your intuition, not your torturous mind. When you experience high stress, intentionally return to your Nine qualities to find your relaxation.

Nine's Growth Type, The Achieving Three, is a natural evolutionary goal for growing Nines, teaching them to be more success-oriented and self-focused, achieving through goals and action. It is tough to reach success when you are too other-oriented, when you divert your attention to either pleasing or avoiding others. Balance for Nines is found by clarifying what you want, putting on blinders, going for the goal, enjoying the accolades, and not settling for anything less than completion.

Nine's Wings - In-Charge Eight & Precise One

Like all the types, Nines have two wings that are very different from the Nine's core nature. The thought of joining the traits of Nine with its in-charge Eight wing may seem unusual, since the qualities of Nine and Eight are seemingly opposite— Nines are indirect and Eights are direct— but these Nines take action by leading with peace. They are generally more outspoken and extroverted than a Nine with a One wing. While still very nice, they emanate greater strength. Like an Eight, they are impulsive at times, have an ability to say no on occasion, and are more easily angered than a Nine with a One wing, though they still have a long fuse. Their Eight-like lust for pleasure makes them more prone to weight gain and almost addictive indulgence.

Nines with a strong One wing are also very pleasant, but with a greater sense of order and values. You're more introverted, reserved, and less prone to speak up until you've got things figured out. You're generally more disciplined than the Nine with a strong Eight wing, holding in your stress and being less impulsive. But while you act from values of right and wrong, you can allow yourself to be stifled by adopting values chosen by others.

Nine's Degrees of Balance

Well-balanced Nines have learned to be individuals, speaking up when necessary and managing conflict, while still being beacons for peace and equanimity. If you're developed, you've taken the necessary risks in life to grow and integrate those traits. You show your individuality, your passion, and go after what you want, while still yielding to find balance with others. Everyone in your caregiving realm benefits.

Average Nines still struggle with being assertive. If you're like most Nines, you have difficulty going after what you want or even identifying what that may be. You want a peaceful environment and tend to avoid situations that aren't. Instead of trying to change the environment to be what you want you tend to tolerate, deny or complain. But if you accept the uncomfortable opportunity of caregiving, the journey can help you to hone your abilities to define and actualize your best self.

Out-of-balance Nines are doormats, living in constant fear of upsetting people and feeling extremely stuck in life, never making moves that make waves. If you felt stuck like this previously in life, you are sure to feel stuck in the care process too. You tend to be anxious and feel you have no options. You just give up, assuming you have to take it. Though you hunger to merge with others, they don't know where you stand and neither do you. You drift through life like a falling leaf, at the beck and call of the wind.

Chapter 19: The Challenger (Type 8)

Fifteen Signs You're a Challenger

You like to be in charge. And why on earth wouldn't anyone put you in charge of things?

You hate, hate, hate to be controlled. In fact, you rarely let this happen to you and anyone who tries is met with a lot of attitude.

Others might accuse you of being domineering.

You have the capacity to work extremely hard in order to manifest your goals.

You are an excellent mentor and can effectively show others how to achieve as you have done, thus nurturing the leaders of the future.

You have a propensity for getting bored very quickly. This can also lead to impatience.

You can come across as somewhat fierce and others can find you intimidating at times.

Anger can be an issue for you and you are inclined to lose your temper fairly easily. Some people find this scary!

As the name of this type implies, you love to take on a challenge and indeed, enjoy giving other people challenges too, thereby helping them to stretch their abilities and even to exceed themselves.

You have an in-built charisma or magnetism. This makes you an effective leader, no matter what sphere you live and work in. You can quite easily persuade others to follow you.

You have great energy and you use this - together with your formidable willpower - to leave your mark on society

You value independence highly and you are not afraid to stand alone, defying social convention if necessary.

You possess a steely determination which others find amazing and sometimes even logic-defying.

You have a powerful 'can do' attitude and tend to be extremely resourceful. You get things done, in a commanding way.

You have an abundance of common sense and this can greatly benefit those around you.

So what do you think? Are you a Challenger? Other people can offer their opinions but only you know for sure.

The Challenger Overview

Control is at the heart of the Challenger's personality. At their core, they are totally unwilling to be controlled, whether it be by a person or by circumstances. It is of the utmost importance to an Eight that they remain the masters of their fates and the captains of their souls. The flip side of this is that they are inclined to be domineering. This coupled with their unwillingness to be controlled may lead them to try to control others. Ironic, is it not? A healthy Challenger is well able to keep this tendency under control but it is something that always has to be guarded against, especially as one moves down the maturity scale. It can be a recurring issue in the interpersonal relationships of an Eight.

Eights take the concept of being strong-willed to new heights. They are tough-minded to a fault and their enormous energy and practical nature aids them significantly in getting their own way.

The Challenger desires to get the most out of life and this can often extend to their physical appetites. They indulge in those appetites without experiencing a hint of unhealthy remorse.

Financial independence is a massive priority for the Challenger. He or she may have difficulty having a boss. They do know best, after all! Challengers tend to benefit from working in a field where they can be their own boss. Under certain circumstances, an Eight may feel the need to opt out of society altogether, finding other ways to gain financial freedom instead, as they are usually uncomfortable with hierarchies.

The Challenger has a deep and abiding fear of feeling vulnerable. This can be detrimental to their capacity to form intimate relationships because, obviously, intimacy requires vulnerability. Defenses need to be lowered! Of course, this involves letting go of the need to be in control and trust is of the greatest importance in this arena. Betrayal of any kind will cut the challenger to the quick. Woe betide the person who violates an Eight in this way!

Believe it or not, Eights can be sentimental. They hide it well, even from those closest to them, but it's true. This is an indication of how much the Eight fears being vulnerable. However, if you do manage to win their trust, you will have someone who stands by you no matter what. The Challenger is hugely protective of those in their inner circle - family and friends especially - and they will move mountains to provide for these people.

A big Achilles Heel for the Eight is their anger. At lower levels of maturity, this emotion can spiral out of control and turn into rage. Such aggression can even turn into violence and unhealthy Eights can be intimidating, ruthless and even dangerous.

Not surprisingly, there are many Eights who have achieved remarkable feats of success in this life. Some examples of these include: Winston Churchill, Oskar Schindler, Martin Luther King, Serena Williams, Barbara Walters, Toni Morrison, Frank Sinatra, Bette Davis, Paul Newman, Richard Wagner, Franklin D. Roosevelt, Fidel Castro, Lyndon Johnson, Golda Meir, Saddam Hussein, Donald Trump, Ernest Hemingway, James Brown, Queen Latifah, Aretha Franklin, Pink, Jack Black, Sean Connery, John Wayne, Mae West, Humphrey Bogart, Jack Black, Dr Phil, Roseanne Barr, Jack Nicholson, Tommy Lee Jones, Clint Eastwood, Lauren Bacall, Chrissie Hynde, Courtney Love, Pablo Picasso, Norman Mailer, Senator John McCain and last but not least, Indira Gandhi.

Conclusion

The Enneagram is an enormous and significant plan for finding out about yourself and other individuals. Like any principal plan, it takes a specific measure of work and time to ace its nuances and complexnesses.

Among the accommodating things about the Enneagram, all the same, is that it starts paying off with profitable experiences when you start investigating it. Since the Enneagram is so tremendous, the information in this book is useful to pay consideration on with a specific end goal to go into this composite assortment of learning.